Public wealth is vast, but largely overlooked as an asset class. Improving its management is one of the most important economic issues of our time. Dag Detter and Stefan Fölster shed much light on the subject. One can only hope that their book will kickstart a debate that ushers in better stewardship of state land, buildings, utilities and other assets. The potential gains are enormous.

MATTHEW VALENCIA, *The Economist*

At a time of mistrust in traditional politics and weak public finances, Dag Detter and Stefan Fölster show politicians the way to demonstrate they are on the side of the people and to manage government assets better. There should be no excuse for those in power to dismiss these ideas.

CHRIS GILES, Economics Editor, *Financial Times*

The Public Wealth of Nations is a very timely reminder of the importance of fiscal transparency and accountability for the sound management of public finances through the often neglected asset side of a government's balance sheet. A very readable and passionate case for governments to focus on their public wealth while taking a long-term view of the implications of their fiscal policies.

MARCO CANGIANO, Assistant Director at the IMF Fiscal Affairs Department and co-editor of *Public Financial Management and Its Emerging Architecture*

The Public Wealth of Nations asks what can be gained by applying lessons from the private sector to the management of public assets. A lot, as it turns out. Many countries continue to ignore the economic return on public assets and focus instead on policy goals of government ownership, or get tangled up in privatization debates. Unsurprisingly, government finances suffer. Using examples from countries such as Sweden and Singapore, the authors show how countries can unlock economic returns, and how government and economic development can benefit. Policy makers and government managers from across the political and development spectrum can learn from this book how the management of assets can truly be in the public interest: by placing financial performance side-by-side with policy objectives.

JIM BRUMBY, Director Governance Global Practice, World Bank

With public finances under pressure in many countries due to a combination of structurally slower growth and high levels of indebtedness, *The Public Wealth of Nations* couldn't be better timed. It is a welcome reminder that the analysis of public finance has hitherto been too narrow, exclusively focusing on debt and its funding costs. In this important book, the authors convincingly argue using many examples that, as with pension funds or even households, an asset-liability approach is needed for public finance as well. They show that intelligent management of public assets can have a huge impact on government revenues, creating room for tax cuts, and on economic growth.

DR. WILLIAM DE VIJLDER, Group Chief Economist, BNP Paribas

Better government handling of public assets is, or should be, a key issue in many countries. With his background as a former president of Stattum, the Swedish government holding company, Dag Detter can speak with great authority and depth of practical experience on the alternative approaches which governments might take. *The Public Wealth of Nations* is an important contribution to a debate of vital concern to governments across the world.

LORD SASSOON, former Commercial Secretary, HM Treasury

Many governments have huge debts, some of which they attempt to hide. Dag Detter and Stefan Fölster show that, rather surprisingly, governments all over the world have hidden valuable real commercial assets that can be monetized in a number of ways: outright privatization, private concessions and more efficient and accountable management of these assets under continued public ownership are just three of these. Efficiency and accountability start with transparency and better information. This important book shows the way forward in turning the latent public wealth of nations into actual riches.

WILLEM H. BUITER, Global Chief Economist, Citi

This insightful book is particularly relevant at a time when public finances are strained and governments are keen to bolster their coffers. Importantly, however, Dag Detter and Stefan Fölster argue that increasing the yield on public assets is not merely another way to boost government revenues. They persuasively argue that a properly designed and politically legitimate stewardship of public assets also confers significant societal benefits, including higher productivity and a more equitable intergenerational distribution of the commons.

LARRY HATHEWAY, Chief Economist Investment Banking

Governments around the world have been acting recklessly in managing their public wealth, which is the key ingredient for securing the welfare of their citizens. This provocative book is a wake-up call for governments to become more responsible in managing their citizens' wealth and securing the foundation for future generations.

MARCEL FRATZSCHER, President of DIW Berlin, Professor at Humboldt-University, and Member of the Advisory Council of the Ministry of Economy of Germany

The debate about the role of the state tends to take place on simplistic terms: Is it good or bad? A more fruitful approach is to ask how to make the state work better. Yet it is hard to have an informed discussion about this because public accounts are woefully primitive: government budgets are generally drawn up on a cash basis and public debts are measured but not public assets. That's where this ground-breaking new book by Dag Detter and Stefan Fölster comes in. It documents how governments have huge assets that they rarely account for, let alone make good use of. And it argues persuasively that if governments of all stripes managed their commercial assets better, they could unlock resources that enhance citizens' welfare. *The Public Wealth of Nations* is a must-read.

PHILIPPE LEGRAIN, visiting senior fellow at the London School of Economics' European Institute and former economic adviser to the President of the European Commission

The Public Wealth of Nations shows how independent public asset governance is an important tool for a more efficient use of society's resources.

RICARDO HAUSMANN, Head of Centre for International Development at Harvard Kennedy School

The Public Wealth of Nations is a must read for policy makers and scholars. It invites readers to think of sovereign wealth in novel ways and brings private solutions to the management of public assets.

ALDO MUSACCHIO, Associate Professor at Harvard Business School and Faculty Research Fellow at NBER

This thought-provoking book shows how unlocking public wealth in the right way can provide a significant boost to the public finances and growth prospects of economies around the world.

ESWAR PRASAD, Senior Fellow at Brookings, Professor at Cornell University, Research Associate at the NBER

Dag Detter and Stefan Fölster have dug up a gold mine of state assets which could be used more profitably and transparently to deliver value for all citizens, including using the revenue to reduce taxes. All it takes is more transparency and better management of such hidden assets. This book deserves much more public awareness of the hidden wealth of nations, often managed incompetently, but sometimes corruptly.

ANDREW SHENG, Distinguished Fellow Fung Global Institute

Governments track their debts to the penny, peso, and yen, yet know surprisingly little about the buildings, businesses, natural resources, and other assets they own. As Dag Detter and Stefan Fölster demonstrate, that neglect creates needless economic harm, and an opportunity for leaders bold enough to correct it. By better managing their assets, governments can enhance transparency, boost growth, and strengthen their fiscal positions.

DONALD MARRON, Director of Economic Policy
Initiatives at the Urban Institute

The Public Wealth of Nations masterfully uncovers the hidden assets of states and convincingly shows how countries can capitalize on their public commercial assets, if only they managed them better. It is a breath of fresh air in these gloomy times of fiscal austerity and public debt pessimism. Detter and Fölster's book should be required reading for policymakers and for every student of public finance.

MATTHIAS MATTHIJS, Assistant Professor of International
Political Economy, Johns Hopkins University (School of
Advanced International Studies)

Dag Detter and Stefan Fölster have made a significant contribution to the discourse on the role of the state in this book. They have assembled a wealth of information on state assets that analysts will find useful while also providing a balanced but compelling argument for a practical-minded approach to unlocking the value of those assets. They identify the drawbacks of state ownership but also offer solutions that would reduce those disadvantages in both developed as well as developing economies.

MANU BHASKARAN, Adjunct Senior Research Fellow at the Lee Kuan
Yew School of Public Policy and founding Director of
Centennial Asia Advisors in Singapore

The Public Wealth of Nations

How Management of Public Assets Can Boost or Bust Economic Growth

The Public Wealth of Nations

Dag Detter

and

Stefan Fölster

First published 2015 by
PALGRAVE MACMILLAN

Palgrave Macmillan in the UK is an imprint of Macmillan Publishers Limited,
registered in England, company number 785998, of Houndmills, Basingstoke,
Hampshire RG21 6XS.

Palgrave Macmillan in the US is a division of St Martin's Press LLC,
175 Fifth Avenue, New York, NY 10010.

Palgrave is a global academic imprint of the above companies and has
companies and representatives throughout the world.

Palgrave® and Macmillan® are registered trademarks in the United States,
the United Kingdom, Europe and other countries.

ISBN: 978–1–137–51984–9

This book is printed on paper suitable for recycling and made from fully
managed and sustained forest sources. Logging, pulping and manufacturing
processes are expected to conform to the environmental regulations of the
country of origin.

A catalogue record for this book is available from the British Library.

Library of Congress cataloging-in-Publication Data

Detter, Dag, 1959-
   The public wealth of nations : how management of public assets can boost or
bust economic growth / Dag Detter, Managing Director of Whetstone and
former President of Stattum, the Swedish government holding company, and a
Director at the Swedish Ministry of Industry, Stefan Fölster, D.phil. from
Oxford University, Director of the Reform Institute in Stockholm and associate
prof. of economics at the Royal Institute of Technology in Stockholm.
      pages cm
   ISBN 978-1-137-51984-9 (hardback)
   1. Finance, Public. 2. Strategic planning. 3. Economic development. I.
Fölster, Stefan. II. Title.
      HJ141.D48 2015
      336--dc23
                                    2015012350

Typeset by Aardvark Editorial Limited, Metfield, Suffolk

Contents

List of figures and tables

Figures

Table

Foreword

It is not every day that you come across a new idea in public policy. After the burst of creativity of the 1990s statecraft is becoming sterile. The left is retreating into the big government ideas of the 1970s. The right is failing to address the great problems of our time such as rising inequality. The left demonizes the use of market mechanisms to improve the state. The right demonizes the use of the state to address market failures. At a time when tech-entrepreneurs are reinventing the world, public policy makers are reinventing the wheel.

The idea of the public wealth of nations is just such a new idea. It identifies a problem that few people had realized exists. It shatters the tired categories of left and right. And it suggests a relatively pain-free way of boosting economic growth.

The argument rests on a striking observation (amply backed up in the text): that governments around the world have billions of dollars of public assets, ranging from corporations to forests to historical monuments, that are usually badly managed and frequently not even accounted for at all. Policy makers have focused on managing debt since the financial crisis of 2007–08. But they have largely ignored the question of public wealth. In most countries public wealth is larger than public debt: managing it better could help to solve the debt problem while also providing the material for future economic growth. Poor management not only throws money down the rat hole. It also forecloses opportunities: the fracking revolution, which is making the US self-sufficient in oil, has taken place almost entirely on private land.

Dag Detter and Stefan Fölster shatter the tired categories of left and right. To right-wing fundamentalists they are dangerous statists. To left-wing diehards they are latter-day Thatcherites. To the rest of us they are brave pragmatists. They argue that the polarized debate between privatizers and nationalizers has missed the point – what really matters is the quality of asset management. The focus when it comes to public wealth should be on yield rather than ownership. They calculate that improvements in public wealth management could yield returns greater than the world's combined investment in infrastructure such as transport, power, water and communications. They also note that improvements in public wealth management could help to win the war against corruption. They thus address at a single stroke two of the great problems of our age: the shortage of infrastructure investment thanks to the overhang of the public debt and the halt in the advance of democracy thanks to the prevalence of bad government.

The Public Wealth of Nations looks in detail at countries that are experimenting with better ways of managing public wealth such as Austria, Finland and Singapore. It also develops a blueprint for better management: vest all state-owned commercial assets in a national wealth fund that can employ the best talents from the private and public sector to manage these assets as effectively as possible. These funds can bring clarity where there is confusion, professionalism where there is amateurism and, as a result, wealth creation where there is wealth destruction. Sensible countries have already outsourced the management of monetary and financial policy to independent central banks and handed control of pension funds to professional fund managers. Creating national wealth funds is the logical next step.

The world is full of problems that seem depressingly difficult to solve: the Greek financial crisis, the deteriorating quality of American infrastructure, the growing demands of the welfare state and the growing unwillingness of taxpayers to pay for them. Better management of public assets provides a relatively easy win in a difficult world. Policy makers of all political persuasions would be foolish to ignore this book.

ADRIAN WOOLDRIDGE

List of abbreviations

ATC	air traffic control
CCP	Chinese Communist Party
CEO	chief executive officer
CFO	chief financial officer
FAA	Federal Aviation Administration (US)
GAO	General Accounting Office (US)
GLC	government-linked company (Singapore)
GSE	government-sponsored enterprise (US)
IMF	International Monetary Fund
IPO	initial public offering
MENA	Middle East and North Africa
MoD	Ministry of Defence (UK)
NBV	net book value
NWF	national wealth fund
OECD	Organisation for Economic Co-operation and Development
PPP	public–private partnership
S&P	Standard & Poor's
SASAC	State-owned Assests Supervision and Administration Commission
SOE	state-owned enterprise
SWF	sovereign wealth fund
TMT	technology, media and telecommunications

chapter 1

What can public wealth do for you?

The single largest owner of wealth in nearly every country is not a private company or an individual like Bill Gates, Carlos Slim, or Warren Buffet. The largest owner of wealth is all of us collectively – you and your fellow taxpayers. And we all have our own personal wealth manager, who we usually call "the government." As far as we can calculate, governments own a larger stock of assets than all very wealthy individuals put together, and even more than all pension funds, or all private equity funds.

What is more, most governments have more wealth than they are aware of, including the many nations caught in the grip of debt crises. Many of these troubled countries own thousands of firms, land titles, and other assets, which they have not bothered to value, let alone manage for the common good. Public wealth is like an iceberg, with only the tip visible above the surface.

For decades, a phony war has raged between those in favor of public ownership and those who see privatization as the only solution. We argue that this polarized debate is partly to blame for neglect of a more important issue – the quality of public asset governance. This makes all the difference to how well public wealth delivers value to its owners – the citizens. Even public assets that are privatized can achieve widely differing outcomes depending on the quality of government regulation, the privatization process, and the competence of private owners. The price for the phony war between privatizers and statists has been lack of transparency, financial waste, and underperformance in the public sector. The only winners are vested interests on both sides of the debate.

In this book, we will argue that how public wealth is governed is one of the crucial institutional building blocks that divides well-run countries from failed states. In fact, the governance of public wealth is not merely a matter of how efficiently state-run companies deliver. Unchecked, public wealth can ruin entire countries and undermine democracy as well. Public wealth can be a curse if it is left as an open cookie jar, tempting its overseers into corruption and clientelism. Even in successful countries like the US, which are, by and large, well organized, public wealth invites democratic perversion that can incite huge policy failures and impose unreasonable hardship and social costs on at least some of its people.

We will argue that democracy is at its best when governments have little direct access to public wealth. This does not mean that all wealth needs to be privatized. The process of privatization itself offers tempting opportunities for quick enrichment, thus risking crony capitalism, outright corruption, or dysfunctional regulation.

We will provide examples of how countries have removed the governance of public wealth from politicians' direct ambit. Freeing governments from having to run public firms changes their mission and focus. Wily politicians will hardly act as consumer activists if they know they are in charge of public companies that fail to deliver, and will have to live up to higher expectations. Freeing politicians from administering public wealth allows them to squarely align themselves with the citizens, formulating expectations, goals, demands, and, where needed, also regulations that attenuate market failures. This goes to the heart of a well-functioning democracy – accountability, transparency, and disclosure.

The most visible public wealth holders are government-owned corporates held by the central government, often called state-owned enterprises (SOEs). Among the world's 2,000 largest companies, SOEs represent 11% of market capitalization of all listed companies worldwide.[1] Several emerging markets, led by Russia and China, have thousands of SOEs. Others, such as Brazil, India, Poland, and South Africa, have several hundred SOEs at the national level. In addition, many countries have thousands of publicly owned corporations at the state/regional and local level.

The central governments of most European countries own dozens or hundreds of large, well-known companies, while countries like Australia and New Zealand have relatively few SOEs. Less visible are the many government-owned corporates, or corporate-like assets owned at a regional and local level. Some of these are proper corporates, but more often they are disguised as various legal entities, but sell commercial services paid for by clients and consumers.

Beyond the corporate organizations owned by governments at different levels lie vast stretches of productive real estate – by far the largest component in public wealth portfolios. More than two-thirds of all public wealth ownership remains opaque – large holdings are owned by local and regional governments or quasi-governmental organizations that are formally independent, but are actually controlled by politician board members. Local savings banks often work like that.

A definition of public wealth

Our definition of public wealth is the sum of the public assets owned by government, namely:

- pure financial assets, such as bank holdings or pension funds
- public commercial assets, such as firms and commercial real estate
- public noncommercial assets, such as roads
- minus government debt.

We use "public" in the financial sense, meaning the wealth owned by various levels of government. It is important to note that "public assets" should not be confused with "public property," which normally refers to assets and resources that are available to the entire public for use, such as public parks.

This book concentrates on public commercial assets, by which we mean assets or operations generating an income (mainly non-tax-based) that could be given some kind of market value if properly structured and used. Typical examples include:

- corporations – typically SOEs
- financial institutions
- real estate
- infrastructure – where toll-based or PPP-related
- noncorporatized commercial activity (e.g. the sale of geographical data or a water utility).

Our definition of public wealth comprises all levels of government – central, regional, and local. However, most statistics or attempts to value public wealth ignore the regional and local level, or capture it only in part.

We generally exclude from our estimates of public assets public noncommercial assets such as national parks, historic buildings, or non-toll-generating roads. Some of the chapters, however, discuss how even these often can be managed in ways that generate higher social value.

Outside our definition of public wealth, we sometimes refer to and discuss quasi-governmental organizations, such as the US home mortgage institutions Fannie Mae and Freddie Mac, or formally independent local savings banks in many countries with local politicians on their boards.

More than 25% of all land in the US is owned by the federal government. Along with all this land, it holds buildings with a book value of $1.5 trillion. In addition, state and local government assets amount to four times these federal holdings, that is, $6 trillion, according to a cautious estimate by the International Monetary Fund.[2]

The US General Accounting Office (GAO), the government spending watchdog, found that "many [federal] assets are in an alarming state of deterioration," noting that the federal government has "many assets it does not need."[3] These include billions of dollars' worth of excess, or vacant buildings. The federal government spends billions of dollars each year maintaining excess facilities in the Departments of Defense, Energy, and Veterans Affairs.

The total worldwide public wealth in government hands, conservatively calculated, is so vast that a higher return of just 1% would add some US$750 billion annually to public revenues.[4] That's a sum equivalent to the GDP of Saudi Arabia. We argue that the professional management of public commercial wealth among central governments could easily raise returns by as much as 3.5%, to generate an extra $2.7 trillion worldwide. This is more than the total current global spending on national infrastructure – for transport, power, water, and communications combined.[5]

In the US, for every 1% increase in yield from the federal government asset portfolio, total taxes could be lowered by 4%. This alone should make every individual citizen, taxpayer, investor, financial analyst, and stakeholder stand up and pay attention. And it should spur demand for action.

As an illustration of the huge difference the governance of public wealth can make, we can look at Panama after the US turned over the management of the Panama Canal Zone in 1977 to the government of Panama. One of the most highly indebted nations in the world at the time now held a potential goldmine. Property within the Canal Zone was an attractive location for many international firms and, in fact, the property value alone at that time was enough to cover Panama's entire national debt. That is, if it had been managed in a professional and commercial way. With a proper focus on value maximization, the Panamanian government could have monetized this attractive asset by renting or selling off attractive parcels. Instead, this opportunity was wasted, with much of the land being overrun by vested interests and used as municipal garbage dumps, informal unregulated housing, and noneconomic military use.[6] In recent years, however, the Panama Canal Authority has become much more efficient and has started to develop the area around the canal, also creating the Colón Free Trade Zone.

Many cities and states in rich countries like the US have similarly mismanaged land holdings that could be an integral part of public finance and used to lower taxes or pay for vital infrastructure. Countries like Greece and Italy, currently in the throes of a financial and fiscal crisis, could use their considerable public assets to help pull themselves out of their bind – without even selling these assets.

Better management is not just about financial returns, but other important social gains as well. Vito Tanzi,[7] an Italian economist, and his co-author Tej Prakash illustrated the misuse of public assets with two examples of schools located in prime property locations, one in Rio de Janeiro, squeezed in between the large hotels on the splendid avenue next to the famous Copacabana beach, and another in the heart of Bethesda, Maryland, established in 1789 when the area was agricultural and the land inexpensive. A relocation of the schools only a few blocks away would bless pupils with a quieter, healthier, and more peaceful study environment. The sale of the more expensive property could be used to hire more teachers.

On top of that, new real estate investment on the current school site would raise national income and tax revenue.

The traditional public sector approach to budgeting almost guarantees the misuse of public commercial assets. Most countries do not have a comprehensive register of public assets (a cadaster). Many governments, be they national, local or regional, would not be able to list, never mind describe, the assets they own and their market value. This makes it difficult to manage these assets in a way that exploits synergies and alternative uses of public assets. Often, decisions are more emotive, such as when, in 1983, President Mitterrand of France decided to move the Ministry of Finance from the Louvre after almost 200 years, to give more space to the Museum of the Louvre.

Alas, all too often, the management of public assets is not conducted in people's best interests. This may come as no surprise in countries where governments are not elected by the people, or are downright kleptocratic. Yet, even democratically run countries rarely take decisions that ideally reflect the people's will or best interests. The institutional governing setup makes all the difference. Greece and Switzerland, for example, are geographically very close and both are democracies. Yet Switzerland, with solid institutions, is one of Europe's richest countries, while Greece is one of the poorest, thanks to dysfunctional institutions.

We argue in this book that democracy has the best chance of working in the public interest when governments are restricted from direct access to public wealth. This does not mean that all wealth must be privatized. The process of privatization itself offers tempting opportunities for quick enrichment, risking crony capitalism, outright corruption, counterproductive regulations, and selling assets at big discounts to placate vested interests.

To some extent, techniques for better management can be borrowed from the best in corporate management. This would include transparency, proper accounting, and realistic balance sheets.[8] We will describe empirical proof that better management techniques make a big difference, and tend to be more common in private firms, especially those that are exposed to competition. Yet, the management of public assets must also work in a political environment, and sometimes respond to social aims beyond financial returns. Much of this book is concerned with analyzing the institutional setups that support the professional governance of public assets by politically steered governments.

The resistance against more commercial governance of public assets shows many similarities with the historical resistance against professional sports. Vested interests long held amateurism in sports as the ideal, until finally, in the early 21st century, the Olympic Games and all the major team sports accepted professional competitors. Today's professionals have taken almost all games to a different level and created a range of multi-billion dollar industries in the process. At the same time, many will probably lament the excesses and misguided incentives that sometimes occur in professional sports. The key in the governance of public wealth is to combine the best of private enterprise management methods with mechanisms that guarantee the pursuit of countries' social aims.

Removing the governance of public wealth from direct government control allows them to concentrate on running their country rather than running a number of public firms. They can then align themselves squarely with consumers and the general public in monitoring performance, and, where needed, implement regulations to attenuate market failures. The holy grail of public commercial asset management is an institutional arrangement that detaches management concerns from direct government responsibility, and simultaneously encourages active governance designed to create greater societal and financial value. Institutional structures that achieve this also help provide a firmer foundation for sound democracy.

In particular, we delve into how some nations successfully manage their commercial assets using professional wealth managers working with a measure of political independence in national wealth funds (NWFs), or similar arrangements. NWFs enable transparency. Debt ratings for these enable independent borrowing that optimizes capital structure and maximizes value. Public listing is also possible, providing the ultimate form of transparency, while broadening the shareholder base and potentially maximizing value to the taxpayer.

Despite the successful examples, only a small percentage of global public commercial assets are managed in these independent and more transparent NWFs, that is, at arm's length from daily political winds. Instead, the vast bulk of public wealth is managed by civil servants inside the government bureaucracy and held in various forms of conglomerates. At best, this is a bureaucratic system designed for handling the allocation of tax money. At worst, it is an arena for political meddling and, occasionally, downright profiteering. Publically owned commercial assets that remain hidden with no transparent economic value are at risk of being whittled away.

The honey trap of public wealth

A common misconception is that a rich state is a strong state. One might think of authoritarian states, such as Russia, where the state controls a third of the local stock market capitalization. Or China, where the government owns four out of five of the Chinese companies on the Fortune 500 list of the world's biggest firms. Yet, while these countries flout powerful state authorities, they can be surprisingly weak in their ability to manage their country in the best interests of the people.[9] For example, 1.2 million Chinese die prematurely every year from air pollution,[10] largely from emissions generated by SOEs.

Some countries with rich and pervasive central governments are what Gunnar Myrdal termed a "soft state."[11] The potential for state action in the common interest is undermined by cadres of state employees who pursue their own agendas. Russia is so much of a soft state that it cannot even produce much economic growth beyond that provided by its oil and gas revenues. At the democratic end of the scale, countries like Brazil find themselves in a similar dilemma, thanks in part to the fact that the state owns a poorly performing third of the country's market capitalization.

In recent decades, many wealthy nations have begun to employ more professional managers and board members in SOEs. But much less progress has been made in establishing professional ownership functions that take responsibility for corporate restructuring, stock offerings for new investments, and other strategic issues. Here, most countries grapple with problems similar to those in Brazil or Russia, but not always as flagrant.

For example, the US Army Corps of Engineers is a federal agency that builds and maintains the infrastructure for ports and waterways. Most of the agency's US$5 billion annual budget goes to dredging harbors and investing in controlling waterway locks and channels, as on the Mississippi River. In addition, the Corps is the largest owner of hydroelectric power plants in the country and manages 4,300 recreational areas, funds beach replenishment, and upgrades local water and sewer systems. The

US Congress has used the Corps as a "pork barrel" spending machine for decades. Funds are earmarked for low-value projects in important members' congressional districts, while high-value projects go unfunded. Unsurprisingly, the Corps has been involved in many scandals, including the levee failures in New Orleans during Hurricane Katrina in 2005, which flooded over 100,000 homes and businesses, led to the deaths of at least 1,833 people, and caused an estimated $100 billion in damage.

Another example is Amtrak, the National Railroad Passenger Corporation, a publicly owned entity operated and managed as a for-profit corporation. Amtrak operates a 22,000-mile nationwide passenger railroad service. Apart from the multiple instances of mismanagement frequently taken up by the GAO, the more costly problem is that state ownership has perverted the democratic process. Amtrak's long-haul routes are deeply unprofitable. Yet maintaining them is necessary for Amtrak to receive the continued support of senators from states that would otherwise lose services. If lossmaking long-haul trains were canceled, Amtrak would serve just 23 states, down from the current 46. That would make it more profitable, allowing it to improve services in areas where it actually has profitable riders. But support from only 23 states is not enough for Congress to keep providing subsidies. Many question why their train tickets often cost much more than an airline flight, despite the more than $30 billion in subsidies Amtrak has received since 1971. This has two important implications. The political deadlock of Amtrak poisons the government's ability to implement an effective railroad or transport policy. Moreover, members of Congress must spend valuable time and energy lobbying to keep Amtrak services to their state.

These examples help illustrate how managing public wealth can pervert democracy, an issue that tends to receive much less attention than the mismanagement of public monopolies. Public wealth within easy reach of governments creates incentives for abuse, for example:

- buying political favors in exchange for lucrative contracts or positions in SOEs
- offering organized interests free access to federal land, or water from public water companies in exchange for political support
- buying the support of unions by allowing higher wage increases in SOEs.

In each of these ways, democracy for the common good degenerates into clientelism. Politicians are rewarded for deftly buying support from various special interest groups rather than enacting reforms that benefit wider public interests. This is the essence of a soft state.

In a clientelist or soft state, governments have little interest in making the management of state assets more transparent. It is hardly an accident that Greece had no consolidated accounts of its considerable state assets, or that the US has no central registry of federal state or local government assets. As long as state ownership stays murky, it is easier for government institutions to distribute favors without scrutiny.

This came back to haunt countries when the financial crisis hit in 2008. No country experiencing financial problems had a remotely true picture of all their public commercial assets. Not only were the assets owned by local or regional governments unknown, but, surprisingly, even central governments had little understanding of their portfolio of assets, its value and yield. Spain and Portugal had both previously pulled together some of their holdings into SEPI (Sociedad Estatal de Participaciones Industriales) and Parpública (Participações Públicas (SGPS) S.A.), respectively, but each held only a fraction of nationally owned assets. Still, this partial consolidation helped to create transparency and save public finances by selling some assets and establishing some creditworthiness with the remainder. Similarly, Ireland set up the National Asset Management Agency in 2009 to manage the bad banking assets from its forced restructuring of the banking sector.

Greece, on the other hand, established a privatization agency with no clout at all. Without a mandate to own any commercial assets, it was reduced to a mere adviser to line ministries, to liquidate assets rather than being allowed to develop and maximize value. With this fragmented approach, ruled by vested interests and crony capitalism, international investors understood that, at best, it would take Greece many years to assess its vast state holdings and be able to reorganize them into productive and valuable assets. What's more, when the government actually produced a consolidated financial review of its commercial asset portfolio, as required by international lenders, publication was stopped.

Those who profit from shady accounting will always argue that revealing the monetary value of public assets will promulgate economistic rather than social aims. We show the opposite to be true. When the value of public assets is revealed, and their managers are told to focus on value creation, then a government can make informed, transparent choices of how much resources to pay SOEs for achieving social aims. Without this transparency, social aims will always be proclaimed by those with selfish agendas.

Even in countries with less outright profiteering, public commercial assets force politicians into a producer mindset. In countries as diverse as Sweden and India, governments have rarely shown any interest in responding to consumer demands for more reliable railway services while being the main owner and provider of train services. Any criticism of state railways threatens to raise questions about government responsibility. As it happens, both countries have mismanaged and grossly underinvested in railroad maintenance for decades. Only when deregulation in Sweden enabled private sector operators to compete did it become politically expedient for the government to pay attention to consumer interests.

This book aims to show that democracy is immensely strengthened when wealth is not at the direct disposal of political control. A strong state is one where politicians must compete with each other over the political agendas intended to promote the common or public interest, rather than competing with promises of dishing out favors that yield access to the public cookie jar.

How countries have removed wealth from political control

In the 1980s and 90s, it became apparent to many that bloated state monopolies often fail to satisfy increasingly sophisticated consumers. Spearheaded by the supply side economics advocated by Ronald Reagan, many countries privatized state firms. Surprisingly, perhaps, the US government only sold a minute share of its public assets. Conrail, a freight rail service, was privatized in 1987, while the Alaska Power Administration and the Federal Helium Reserve were privatized in 1996. The Elk Hills Naval Petroleum Reserve was sold in 1997, and the United States Enrichment Corporation, which provides enriched uranium to the nuclear industry, was privatized in 1998. These were all small entities. More significantly, a number of countries worldwide, including several countries like Sweden under social democratic governments, divested a significantly larger percentage of state assets and began managing remaining state-owned assets more professionally.

Privatization is one way of placing public wealth out of easy reach of politicians. But it also opens pitfalls. If the privatized state firms are monopolies or financial institutions, smart regulation is usually required to force them to act in consumers' best interests. Without well-designed regulation, there may be a backlash in public opinion. The privatization process itself is a challenge in countries prone to corruption and crony capitalism.

Some countries have taken broader steps than simply privatizing a few businesses. The recent book, *Renaissance for Reforms*, analyzed 109 rich national governments and found that when an incumbent government implemented ambitious market-oriented reforms, they were also more likely to be re-elected.[12] Even more surprising, perhaps, is that this reward for reforms tends to be most pronounced for governments seen to be on the left.

In many cases, ambitious market-oriented reforms came in waves, moving slowly from a clientelist political culture toward placing the common good above demands from special interests. A good example of this was Canada in 1993 when Paul Martin was appointed minister of finance in the newly elected center-left Liberal Party government. Canada had been running deficits close to 7% of GDP at the time, and the following year gross national debt exceeded 100% of GDP. Martin realized that real change was needed for the country to reverse its deepening debt spiral. David Herle, at the time an adviser to Martin, and his co-author John Springford, related in the *Financial Times* the difficulties involved in introducing reforms in early 1990s' Canada.[13] According to Herle and Springford, a rare cabinet ally to the minister of finance was Ralph Goodale, minister of agriculture. But their friendship took a turn for the worse when Goodale, raised on the Canadian prairie and representing a wheat-growing Saskatchewan farm district, strongly opposed Martin's proposal to abolish the so-called "Crow Rate" – a system of wheat transport subsidies. What's more, the agricultural minister wasn't the only person upset by reduced expenditures. Large segments of the Canadian Liberal Party resented the reforms, as did many organizations and businesses whose public subsidies were affected. The drastic market reforms were tough medicine for them to swallow.

The Canadian reforms included privatizing several government-owned corporations and instituting more professional management in others. This strategy moved the nation toward what can be described as a new social contract. Short term, these changes seemed to upset several interest groups, businesses, and families. Still, the Canadian Liberal Party won a second term of majority rule in 1997. Following another term of reform policies, it again won the election in 2000. Over this period, the party shifted from describing its growth-oriented reforms as an emergency response to crisis, and instead promoted them as long-term reforms designed to create a better society. *The Wall Street Journal* and the Heritage Foundation have published a report annually on the degree of economic freedom in the world since 1995. Their 2013 Index of Economic Freedom report stated that: "Canada's economic freedom score is 79.4 [out of 100, the theoretical maximum], making its economy the 6th freest" in the world, compared to the 12th place ranking for the US. In 2014, Canada passed the 80 point score level, while still ranked sixth, it joined the highest level of economic freedom – "free."

In other countries that similarly revamped their economies, including Australia and Sweden, reforming SOEs had a much wider effect on the economy than simply improving productivity within each enterprise. When an SOE was either privatized or put under more professional management, it was also natural for politicians to open up the whole sector to competition. This drove structural change, sometimes with dramatic consequences. When telephone companies lost their monopolies, the mobile phone and Internet access markets took off in a way that would not otherwise have been possible.

Privatization is not always necessary to dramatically improve asset management. Even in market-oriented Netherlands, SOEs account for 5% of market capitalization of the local stock market. In 1998, Sweden changed direction and decided to become an active owner of its central government-owned commercial assets, with value maximization as the sole objective, along with proper transparency, appointing professional boards, and setting relevant targets for dividend yield and capital structure on a par with its private sector competitors, aiming to follow national wealth pioneers in Austria and Singapore. After a few years, however, Sweden partially retreated, taking a more hands-off approach to governing SOEs. This is convenient for politicians wanting to avoid taking operational decisions they could be blamed for. Yet it turned out to be insufficient to ensure success.

Without a proper institutional framework and governance allowing for a professional management, or governance, these firms were often left as "orphans." At one end of the spectrum, profitable companies were left with no controls on their surpluses, allowing for uncontrolled investment expansion into foreign markets. At the other end, unprofitable organizations with ballooning operational costs were left unreformed, sometimes serving mainly to provide tax-subsidized employment. As we show in more detail later, better management within SOEs can still lead to spectacular failures if professional governance is neglected.

Toward better governance of public wealth

In our view, the best way to foster good management and democracy is to consolidate public assets under a single institution, removed from direct government influence. This requires setting up an independent ring-fenced body at arm's length from daily political influence and enabling transparent, commercial governance.

A similar international trend has been to outsource monetary and financial stability to independent central banks. A central bank is a deposit for reserves and a source of revenue from profits gained from creating money. Easy cash also renders central banks tempting for politicians seeking a quick fix. In blatant cases, a government will force its central bank to print too much money, eventually leading to hyperinflation. Even in many well-run countries, though, government meddling has consistently led to excessive money creation or excessively low interest rates. Following the inflationary 1970s and 80s, the most common response among OECD countries was to make central banks independent of short-term government influence, vesting the responsibility for the institution with a board, nominated and approved by the legislative branch, or parliament, and given a long-term mandate.

Independent central banks were controversial in many countries when introduced. In particular, trade unions were worried they would punish negotiated wage increases with higher interest rates, and criticized the idea as undemocratic. Over time, however, experience with independent central banks has been positive and has been widely copied.

The main argument in this book is that similar reforms of public wealth governance can bestow significant economic and democratic benefits. We also show how some countries have fared after putting the management of public pensions and assets in so-called "bad banks" out of easy reach of government meddling. A few countries have placed most public wealth in holding companies or funds with remarkable independence. We use the term national wealth funds (NWF) for these institutions for independent governance of public commercial assets. As with independent central banks, NWFs do not offer a watertight guarantee of better management in kleptocratic governments. But they would help most countries that are trying to make their democratic institutions more robust. Even stable democracies stand to gain much from more professional governance of their assets.

This book provides an in-depth look at the economic arguments in favor of governing public commercial assets more effectively and the tools available to do so, while emphasizing the importance of proper regulation. We make head-to-head comparisons between success stories in contrasting systems – Singapore, Abu Dhabi, China, Austria, Finland, the UK, and Sweden – providing a variety of examples for what has worked and what has not. Interestingly, a few Asian countries now have state-of-the-art governance of state assets.

Our proposals extend beyond the governance of just commercial assets. An NWF with sufficient independence from government control could be allowed to rebalance its portfolio and not only help finance infrastructure investments, but also act as the professional steward and anchor investor in newly formed infrastructure consortia. This could mean that an NWF could be a great boon to investment in much needed infrastructure.

In the aftermath of the financial crisis, many countries remain heavily indebted and fettered by fiscal austerity, attempting to restore budgetary balance and thereby economic growth. Policy choice is confined to saving more, either now or later. Structural labor market reforms and competition rules are also on the cards, but these can take years to nudge growth and employment rates in the right direction.

When people describe the economic situation of a country, they often ignore an essential element. Most European countries own huge portfolios of commercial assets, as do both federal and local governments in the US. The value of these public portfolios may be even larger than the corresponding public debts in each country, but governments rarely possess the detailed information needed to understand the extent of their own wealth. Even heavily indebted countries like Greece may be asset rich. This is why we should start asking: "What can public assets do for the economy?"

Don't bite the hand that feeds you: the cost of poor governance

Anyone flying from an American airport to any of the many newly built airports in Asia, or even some of the privately held airports in Europe, cannot help but notice a remarkable difference. The shoddy appearance of many American airports is not, in fact, a sign of thrift. Quite the opposite. Nearly all major US airports are owned by state or local governments that receive federal governmental subsidies for renovation and expansion. This mixing of responsibilities is in itself an obstacle to efficient management. But it does not stop there. Numerous federal roadblocks make cities hesitant to privatize. For example, government-owned airports can issue tax-exempt debt, which gives them a financial advantage over potential private competitors.

By contrast, many thriving airports around the world have been fully or partially privatized, even in Europe. This long list includes Athens, Auckland, Brussels, Copenhagen, Frankfurt, London, Melbourne, Naples, Rome, Sydney, and Vienna. Britain led the way with the 1987 privatization of the British Airports Authority, owner of Heathrow and other airports.

Even without privatization, more efficient public management could accomplish obvious improvements, for example increasing income from commercial activities and renting out space more efficiently and in a more attractive way to private vendors. The captive audience of an airport is an ideal client base and a good source of revenue for commercial interests, and attractive vendors tend to be appreciated by travelers with spare time.

Thus, a properly incentivized owner, private or public, that can manage an airport professionally can earn a much better return than many American airports currently achieve.

American airports are only one small example of the unintended consequence of poor public enterprise governance. In many emerging market economies, however, SOEs have been used as a tool for national ambitions. Some of the largest and fastest expanding multinationals are government-owned companies in China, Russia, and many other countries. They increasingly compete with private firms and other SOEs for resources, ideas, and export contracts. A January 2013 special issue of *The Economist*, "The rise of state capitalism," argued that: "The spread of a new sort of business in the emerging world will cause increasing problems." SOEs have always been an important element of most national economies, but these were often confined to domestic markets and lagged behind in business performance.

This chapter describes how commercial state-owned assets are managed, and then compares this to management in private firms. Research indicates that growing state-owned sectors, traditionally governed, can impose a significant cost on consumers.

State capitalism: renaissance and backlash

Sentiments toward the more visible side of public commercial assets, the corporates and banks owned at a central government level – the SOEs – have swung back and forth. This polarized debate between statists and privatizers has detracted attention from the main question – the quality of asset governance.

European governments nationalized firms after World War II, but in the 1970s this trend grew in force, in the belief that this would boost economic growth, employment, and perhaps political power. This model was emulated by governments in many developing countries. By the end of the 1970s, in many countries the share of national output from SOEs outweighed that generated by large private firms. In many cases, an even larger share of the economy came from the ownership of a wider portfolio of public commercial assets at the local and regional level.

Today, more than 30 years after the Thatcher/Reagan privatization drive, and with state socialism abandoned all over Europe, a common myth in western countries may be that government ownership of commercial assets is ancient history.[1] But the reality is quite different, albeit concealed by scanty accounting. For example, the most recent official statistics of the number of SOEs in Germany were published as far back as 1988. At the end of 1988, the country had 3,950 companies owned by the federal or local governments, equaling 16.7% of gross fixed capital formation and employing 9.2% of all employees – with a concentration in the postal and rail services, utilities, credit institutions, and insurance companies.

In the following years, some companies were sold while others are now listed on the stock market, although still government controlled, as with the Deutsche Bundespost, the federal postal service, in 1995. Researchers at the University of Potsdam tried to reassess the amount of state ownership and, in 2006, they found close to 10,000 government-owned firms in Germany, on all levels, including federal, regional, and local. When the OECD later initiated a study to assess the size of SOE portfolios in each member country, the German government did not participate or support the study.

The continuing plethora of state-owned firms in Germany and many countries may be surprising. After all, between the 1970s and 2000, countries have sold off many state firms and tried to modernize the management of the ones they kept, with corporate governance reforms, performance contracts for firms and managers, and training programs for SOE executives. They tried to create a level playing field for private sector competitors that were now able to compete with these former monopolies.

But in the early years of the 21st century, prior to the financial crisis of 2007, state capitalism rebounded, this time mainly in the emerging markets. Plans for complete privatization were scrapped. Instead, minority holdings of SOEs were sold to private investors. For example, Chinese SOEs were floated in Hong Kong, Shanghai, and New York. Seemingly unconcerned by government control, investors poured more than $100 billion into the largest 20 IPOs (initial public offering) alone. These ranged from construction firms to banks and railways. In India, the government sold shares in Coal India, a dinosaur with a vast array of open pit mines. Even Indonesia and Malaysia introduced a range of public assets on the stock exchange.

By 2014, the picture had changed dramatically again. Asia's 65 largest SOEs have lost a trillion dollars in value since their peak in 2007, much more than private firms, while their share of Asian companies' market value fell from well above to well below half the total. And their aggregate price-to-earnings ratio is nearly half that of private firms. Investors became highly skeptical of buying into partially state-owned firms.[2] Worldwide, the share of large listed SOEs in global market capitalization has been cut nearly in half from a peak of 22% in 2007. Between 2007 and 2014, the SOEs among the world's top 500 firms have lost between 33% and 37% of their value.[3] Global shares as a whole rose by 5%.

In part, these whims of investors reflect overall stock market trends. But the new dim view of state-owned firms prevailed even as stock markets in the US and Europe soared in 2013 and 2014. Moreover, SOEs ran into other kinds of trouble. Investors have become increasingly wary of state meddling, graft (the unscrupulous use of a politician's authority for personal gain), and the simple risk that SOEs are outcompeted by nimbler rivals. NTT DoCoMo, the Japanese state-controlled mobile phone operator, has struggled to keep up with savvier private rivals. State-owned banks in China that dominate the market are being outsmarted by private rivals that offer higher returns on savings accounts.

Further, investors may have become suspicious of the relationship between SOEs and the financial crisis. The imperative question they ask: "Is it a coincidence that some of the worst hit countries in the financial crisis, such as Greece and Italy, were among the highest ranked nations for owning SOEs in the world just prior to the crisis, which sorely exposed the economic and political weakness of their economies" (see Figure 2.1)? Why did countries like Australia, New Zealand, and Poland do so much better? Here, Spain, also clobbered by the financial crisis, seems to be the odd man out. In truth, however, Spain only appears to have few SOEs because many of its problem banks were local savings banks, not officially counted as SOEs.

The follow-up question is then: Could it be that a large state-owned sector hides productivity problems and reduces pressure to implement growth reforms?

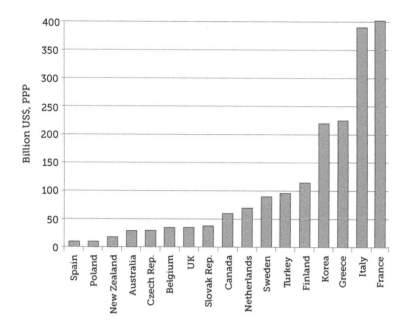

FIGURE 2.1 Asset value of central government SOEs in OECD countries, 2003
Source: OECD questionnaire on corporate governance of state-owned enterprises, 2003; OECD in Figures

Common arguments for public wealth

In light of these suspicions, why do governments bother with administering a wide array of public assets? The case for public ownership essentially rests on the presumption that the people are not always capable of contracting individually with private firms to achieve socially beneficial outcomes. Some of the frequently stated aims are:

- *Industrial policy:* through a government-owned enterprise, the state may be able to launch emerging industries, save declining industries, or help the private sector carry greater risk.
- *Development:* to help develop poorer regions through investment in infrastructure or new production plants.
- *Fiscal policy and redistributive goals:* as when national post office services charge monopoly prices for delivery in cities in order to subsidize postal distribution in rural areas.
- *Environmental goals and protection of national heritage.*

For South Korea, Turkey, and Mexico, direct state intervention was justified with national developmental goals. Similarly, many European countries and Japan nationalized companies or established national companies after World War II – especially in the energy, transport, and banking sectors – hoping that this would aid efforts to rebuild the economy.

Economists have specified a range of more fundamental arguments for how public assets can conceivably spur growth or mitigate market failures. One such theoretical argument is that state intervention can ameliorate the consequences of a natural monopoly, where economies of scale allow the monopolist to thwart the competition with lower prices and still earn large profits. This can occur in the power generation, gas, and railway sectors – all cases where an interlocking supply network is required to provide goods or services. In this situation, a private firm may engage in monopoly pricing.

Even state monopolies, however, may abuse their pricing power. Many countries have tried regulation to avoid this, or even forced firms to split and spin off their downstream operations. For example, the state may run the rail infrastructure network, but encourage competing private providers to operate the various transport services.

A second kind of market failure might occur in the production of so-called "public goods" that can be used even by those who choose not to pay. Third, in some cases, consumers cannot afford to pay, which is a commonly stated argument for public schools.

Some activities cause externalities, both positive and negative side effects that impact other people. Information asymmetry is also used to justify state intervention. This occurs when important information in a market is only available to some, leaving others to second-guess and perhaps refrain from participating.

These possible market failings can motivate state intervention. But they do not prove that interventions succeed. Even state action may lead to failures of information, fall victim to bureaucratic motives in conflict with social optimality, and cause flaws in the workings of democracies. In such circumstances, the outcome of state intervention may be worse than market-based outcomes even in the face of market failures.

State capitalism has sometimes appeared to successfully produce national champions that can compete globally. Two-thirds of emerging market companies that made it to the Fortune 500 list in 2014 are state owned, and most of the rest enjoy state support of some kind. Typically, they get various types of government help in reaching global markets, such as low-cost financing from state-owned banks. A lingering suspicion is that when SOEs occasionally outcompete their rivals, it may often be by accepting lower rates of return or taking greater risks at taxpayers' expense. For that reason, the treatment of SOEs is also a bone of contention in the ongoing Trans-Pacific Partnership negotiations.

Brazil's Vale, for example, considers itself a private sector mining company, but the national government treats it as a government-owned national champion, because three "golden shares" belong to the Brazilian government, apart from a significant holding by the national pension funds. These recently forced Vale's boss, Roger Agnelli, to step aside because they did not like his plans to sack workers.

Similarly, China's Lenovo likes to portray itself as a private sector computer company, but the Chinese Academy of Sciences, a government institution controlled by the Chinese Communist Party (CCP), provided it with seed money (and still owns a large share of the company as a parent), and the government has repeatedly stepped in to smooth its growth, not least when it acquired IBM's personal computer division for US$1.25 billion in 2004. At the beginning of 2014, Lenovo, now the world's largest personal computer maker, announced that it would acquire IBM's industry standard x86 server business valued at US$2.3 billion in cash and stock.[4] The deal was completed in October. In the same month, it completed its US$2.91 billion acquisition of Motorola Mobility from Google, to continue its expansion in the global smartphone market.[5]

In fact, the CCP remains an omnipresent factor in the Chinese economy, not least through its Organization Department, which controls the appointment of the three main executives in an SOE. Its influence at a regional and local level is even greater, with provincial officials controlling the much larger number of appointments in regional and local corporations. In a penetrating analysis, Richard McGregor unveils how a long list of "national champions" operates in the shadow of the state, including Geely in cars, Huawei in telecoms equipment, and Haier in white goods, all with an opaque ownership structure and party connections that enable them to benefit from the cheap capital that the CCP makes available to potential national champions.[6] This makes the CCP and its leaders extremely influential, presiding over the largest concentration of commercial assets in the world.

In fact, SOEs account for between one-third and one-quarter of Chinese GDP. Yet, their success can be questioned. According to a revealing book by Nick Lardy, state capitalism in China is almost a complete failure, with the return on SOE assets being extremely low, not even half the cost of capital.[7] This makes them a drag on China's economic growth. SOEs are, however, less common in the manufacturing sector, which partly explains the success of Chinese industry. But they are prevalent in vital service sectors such as telecoms, business and leasing services, and transportation. If Chinese economic growth has been impressive, it is despite, not because of, its SOEs.

After these theoretical arguments and anecdotal descriptions, it is time to survey the evidence. As we shall see, the research literature does not generally support the notion that state-owned champion firms are conducive to growth.

Management of state-owned enterprises

Comparisons between state-owned and private firms are often misleading, since SOEs are frequently monopolies, quasi-monopolies, or sole providers to consumers and can charge higher prices. Many state-owned companies were also buoyed by the boom in prices for natural resources for which they often have exclusive rights.

Occasionally, monopoly profits may be diluted by state-mandated services. State-owned postal services in many countries, for example, have a monopoly on the distribution of mail, but also an obligation to serve rural areas that entail losses – the universal service obligation. For these reasons, rates of return from SOEs are not a sufficient metric of the efficiency of the state as an owner if they cannot be benchmarked against private sector competitors.

Over recent decades, economists have instead used productivity and other efficiency measures to compare public and private firms, controlling for various sources of error. This large theoretical and empirical literature indicates that, on average, SOEs tend to be less efficient than their private counterparts.[8]

Nevertheless, a caveat is in order. Not all studies find statistically significant differences, although most do. Comparisons may also be blurred because SOEs often manage to increase efficiency when the likelihood of being privatized increases. For example, a South Korean study found that the efficiency of South Korean SOEs increased significantly from 1998 to 2002 when the new government signaled its intention to privatize many of them.[9] This, and similar results in other studies, strongly supports our contention that SOEs can be managed much better even when they are not (yet) privatized.

A common explanation in this literature for the inefficiency of state ownership – the agency view – is that managers of SOEs lack high-powered incentives and are not properly monitored by active owners or the market. An alternative hypothesis is that less efficient firms are more likely to have been nationalized in the first place. A key factor in some of these studies appears to be the degree of competition. Where SOEs face competitive environments, they sometimes perform equally as well as private firms.[10] Also, SOEs seem to perform as well as private firms when they follow the management and corporate governance practices used in private firms.

Recent research has provided empirical insight into why SOEs perform worse on average. Analyzing management has traditionally relied on case studies, which, by their nature, provide anecdotal rather than empirical proof. But, over the past decade, Nicholas Bloom and John van Reenen began surveying management practices in tens of thousands of firms, using a method for describing management practices originally developed by McKinsey.[11] The central elements of this survey are the extent to which firms measure and follow targets, provide their employees with incentives, manage human capital, and other similar factors.

A key finding of Bloom and van Reenen is that management practices are clearly linked to outcomes. Not only are firms that follow best practice more productive and profitable, the connection is convincing in many other respects as well. For example, hospitals with better management practices have higher survival rates. Management practices vary considerably across organizations, countries, and sectors, but tend to mirror the spread of performance. One factor linked to this variation is ownership.

Government, family, and founder-owned firms are more often found to be poorly managed, while multinational, dispersed shareholder, and private equity-owned firms are more often well managed. Stronger product market competition and higher worker skills are associated with better management practices. Bloom and van Reenen find that less regulated labor markets are associated with improvements in incentive management practices such as performance-based promotion.

These studies provide insights into the problem every government faces in managing their companies. Frequently, these companies are not fully exposed to market competition. In many cases, there is also a sense that the company will be bailed out with taxpayer money if it performs poorly. Either way, the challenge is to instill a sense of urgency among management in SOEs to adopt best management practices. Confronting this challenge is an uphill battle if politicians meddle unduly in day-to-day company decisions. The key question, to which we will return in later chapters, is how a government can go about ensuring active and professional governance without risking opportunistic meddling.

Are SOEs really good for growth?

If SOEs are managed less well than other firms, wouldn't that mean that countries with more SOEs also perform less well economically? Generally, one wouldn't expect that kind of relationship to be easy to determine. Statistics on state ownership are of poor quality, with few countries to study and the potential for large measurement errors. Firms owned by local and regional governments or state-controlled foundations are usually not even considered. Most important, perhaps, is the theoretical nature of the expected relationship. SOEs would not necessarily be expected to have lower productivity growth even if they adopt worldwide technological progress with some delay, but a lower productivity level than comparable private firms. If that is true, a country with many SOEs might have lower GDP rather than lower growth. We would then expect countries that divest themselves of SOEs to grow faster than countries that increase state holdings instead. This, in turn, raises additional demands on data quality. It is not enough to measure public ownership in any single year, but rather requires tracking change over time.

In addition, GDP growth is influenced by many factors that must be controlled for. Kapopoulos and Lazaretou, two economists, do this well, using ownership data for samples of firms in 27 high-income countries in 1995.[12] After controlling for several variables, they found that countries that have a higher share of SOEs clearly experience lower growth. We have tried to repeat this exercise for more recent years and using different data. The OECD surveyed wholly or partially state-owned firms in 34 countries in 2008, 2009, and 2012.[13] Unfortunately, firms can be valued many ways and countries use different standards.

An alternative approach is therefore based on the number of employees in central government SOEs as a percentage or share of total employment. Among OECD countries this varies from 0.5 to 12%, averaging about 3%. The highest value is in Norway, which has many state-owned assets, including its globally ranked oil giant, Statoil. The Finnish central government also owns many large firms, including the power generator Fortum, the airline Finnair, and Neste Oil. In contrast, state ownership is very low in Australia, Canada, and South Korea. Figures 2.2 and 2.3 illustrate the average share per country over the years surveyed and the change.

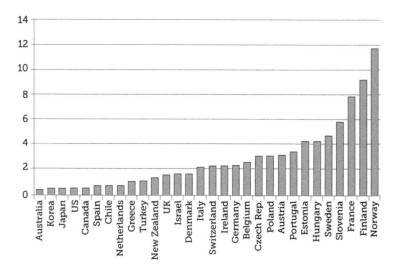

FIGURE 2.2 Workers employed by SOEs, as percentage of total employment
Sources: OECD; see Christiansen (2011) for details on data collection

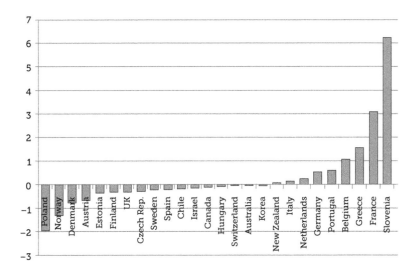

FIGURE 2.3 Change in SOE employment as share of total employed in SOEs, 2008–12, percentage change from base year 2008

Sources: OECD; see Christiansen (2011) for details on data collection

There seems to be little correlation between the prevalence of SOEs in countries and the GDP per capita level, as Figures 2.4 and 2.5 illustrate. The top figure in Figure 2.4, for richer OECD countries, seems to show a positive correlation, but this is actually caused by a single outlier, Norway. Excluding Norway, the correlation turns negative.

Looking instead at the relationship between changes in total size of state-owned sectors and GDP growth, a different picture arises. Figure 2.5 illustrates that divesting state-owned companies seemingly correlates negatively with growth. This, too, is a naive correlation that should be treated with caution, in particular because of the financial turbulence in the years after 2008.

In order to explore the naive correlation a bit further, we have made the analysis more systematic, by controlling for national employment rates, population size, GDP, and educational standards.[14] In this regression, the prevalence of SOEs has a negative, significant relation to economic growth. On average, a 1 percentage point increase in state-owned firms' share of total employment between 2008 and 2012 corresponds to a per capita GDP decrease of $132 over the four-year period 2009 to 2013. This can be compared to average growth during the same period, which was $909. Put differently, increasing the share of employment in state-owned firms by 5 percentage points would wipe out three years of growth, on average.

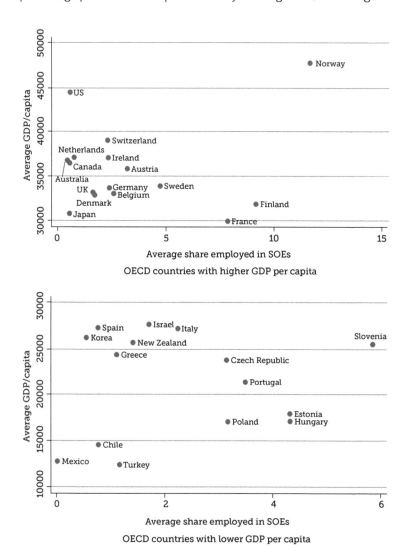

FIGURE 2.4 National GDP and SOE employment as share of total employed
Sources: OECD; authors' calculations

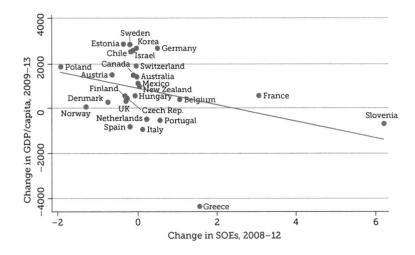

FIGURE 2.5 Correlation between change in GDP per capita and SOE employment as share of total employed

Sources: OECD; authors' calculations

Such a regression is hardly proof of causality, which remains both empirically and conceptually rather elusive. The politics that lead governments to acquire or sell firms are themselves influenced by a wide variety of changes in and to society that may also correlate to growth. Given the limitations of the data, we do not intend to draw strong conclusions from these regressions on their own, although they seem to be corroborated by the earlier study of Kapopoulos and Lazaretou (2005). Yet they do indicate that macroeconomic correlations are consistent with microeconomic research, pointing to poorer management in SOEs that we reviewed earlier in this chapter.

A crucial question is whether poor governance of public assets can have wider detrimental effects on a country's development beyond what becomes manifest in the SOEs themselves. We turn to this in Chapter 3.

chapter 3

How poorly governed state-run businesses can ruin the economy and politics

It would be natural to think that large public wealth helps a government to steer a country well. Paradoxically, the opposite seems to be the case. Just as a country may suffer from the "Dutch disease" when blessed with an abundance of natural resources, public wealth can have toxic side effects. A "public wealth malaise" is hardly caused by incompetence among politicians, even if some businesspeople like to think so. The disease transcends how well the state-owned firms are managed. Rather, the public wealth malaise comes about because the administration of public wealth seriously distracts politicians from their primary task and, indeed, mandate – to promote the common good. In fact, more public wealth weakens governments and democratic decision making.

Three main mechanisms come into play when public wealth perverts democracy. These are, first, corruption, outright illegal bribes, or embezzlement for private gain. Second, clientelism – politicians favoring their supporters in return for votes or other favors. And third, the conflict of interest that arises when politicians are in charge of production instead of representing and voicing consumer interests.

Corruption and crony capitalism

In spring 2014, Song Lin, boss at China Resources, one of the world's largest state-owned conglomerates, was placed under investigation and later removed, accused of corruption. This event was notable, not because corruption surrounding SOEs is unusual, but because such corruption cases are so rarely exposed. In fact, there is a lot of evidence suggesting that SOEs in many countries are a tool for the enrichment of a chosen political class. The OECD's (2014) first report on international bribery analyzed 400 international bribery cases. One of the conclusions was that most bribes go to managers of SOEs, closely followed by customs officials.

Other interesting research literature ties corruption to excessive regulation and red tape. For example, Goel and Nelson (1998) show that, in American states, more corruption goes hand in hand with larger state government. And causation may go both ways. Many who profit from corruption appear to propagate an even larger state. Another study, published in the *Public Administration Review*, finds that states with more corrupt government officials often have more state-run activities directed toward areas where it is easier to be corrupt.[1]

Countries with many SOEs are also rife with corruption. According to Forbes, the top 50 members of China's National People's Congress boast a combined wealth of $94.7 billion, making their American congressional cousins – whose top 50 members are worth only $1.6 billion – look poor in comparison.[2] Of the 358 Chinese billionaires on the Hurun China Rich List, 90 are active politicians.

During 2014, China arrested thousands of public officials for corruption. This campaign reached into the very top of the Chinese Communist Party (CCP), bringing the arrest of Zhou Yongkang, the most senior Chinese official investigated since the Gang of Four (which included Jiang Qing, the late leader Mao Zedong's last wife) in the early 1980s. Until 2012, Zhou had been a member of the Politburo Standing Committee that runs China. Perhaps more importantly, he was the former head of state security in control of the courts, police, and intelligence agencies, and said to control the Chinese oil industry and, as such, one of the most powerful men in China.

While private sector wrongdoing was energetically exposed in this campaign, investigators had largely been soft on state-backed businesses. Xi Jinping, the new premier, appears to be changing tack by attacking his own elite and asserting his own grip on national power within the heart of political leadership, as well as the powerful business leadership.

Deng Xiaoping became the CCP's de facto chief in 1978, and in the next two and a half decades much of the state sector was privatized. But this trend has almost totally come to a halt in the past 10 years. For example, in every year since 2005, state-controlled oil and financial institutions, mostly banks, have accounted for three-fifths to four-fifths of all profits earned by companies listed on Chinese stock markets. The state connection enables companies owned by the government to dominate every market where profits can be made: from telecoms to tobacco, and insurance to infrastructure. The state has liberalized certain sectors – retail, services, agriculture, and low-end manufacturing – but these are fiercely competitive sectors with tight margins. Sadly, opportunities for graft may be the most important reason why Chinese politicians like to keep profitable businesses in state hands.

In fact, corruption in China has worsened dramatically over the past year. In 2014, China was ranked at number 100, down from 80 the year before, and tied with Algeria and Suriname in the annual Transparency International Corruption Perceptions Index of 175 countries, which ranks states from least to most corrupt.

In India, too, politicians apparently like to keep SOE profits within easy reach. In August 2014, Indian investigators arrested S.K. Jain, the head of the state-owned Syndicate Bank, accusing him of taking an $82,000 bribe to increase credit limits for two companies being probed in a scandal involving the allocation of coal mining blocks under the previous national government. Known as the "Coal scam," this is among the largest corruption cases to tarnish the Congress-led national coalition government, which lost the election in May 2014 after a decade in power. Two years previously, the official auditor said the government had lost over $33 billion in potential revenue by transferring coal mining blocks too cheaply to private companies. The Syndicate Bank, founded in southern India in 1925, was nationalized in 1969 and is now 67% state owned, although it is listed on the Bombay Stock Exchange. Jain had been a banker for nearly three decades, having moved from the Bank of Baroda (another state-controlled institution) to take charge of Syndicate Bank in July 2013. Government-owned banks dominate the Indian banking sector.

Opportunities for graft are particularly rife in sectors that, by their nature, require government licensing, such as natural resource extraction. This works both ways. Once bureaucrats and politicians benefit from the opportunities for graft arising from licensing and other administrative complexities, they also become a forceful constituency for maintaining red tape or making it even more complex. In many cases, natural resources are also public assets that governments can make available to private sector investors of their choosing. This is an open invitation to crony capitalism. Sometimes, governments choose to exploit natural resources in SOEs, which may make things even worse, as the above-mentioned OECD study claims. It is likely no coincidence that Russia has an exceptionally large number of billionaires in exactly the same sectors that are dominated by SOEs, such as Gazprom, the world's largest extractor of natural gas.

Wealth attracts those seeking wealth. Large public wealth may attract the type of politician who is more prone to corruption. Political leaders can be tempted to use public wealth in ways that direct bribes their way, while also enriching the people paying the bribes. Unfortunately, this tends to impoverish everyone else. Indeed, this is reminiscent of how medieval kings controlled their nations – granting nobility access to public wealth. And, sadly, this is still the way many countries are governed today – Russia, China, and India are not the only, or even the worst, examples.

Corruption may amount to nothing more than a transfer of income if politicians take bribes mainly to facilitate processes that would otherwise become mired in red tape. But graft is a serious burden to development when bribes are taken for actions that harm national development, or if red tape is increased simply to create more opportunities for bribes. Even earlier in US history, corruption in connection with state intervention was an issue. State governments have frequently intervened in infrastructure projects, such as canals and railroads, but this intervention often ended in corruption scandals.[3]

Vast public assets by themselves do not necessarily turn a country corrupt. But a milder form of legal corruption is common even in advanced democracies.

Clientelism

In tribal societies, political leaders need support from a sufficient number of tribes, which is done through political largesse in exchange. This way of ruling a country makes it paramount for a political leader to control significant public wealth. In modern societies, "tribes" have been replaced, in most cases, by interest groups. Leaders who secure support from interest groups can reduce public criticism or scrutiny. Collecting support from enough interest groups often involves catering to their demands on specific issues. A recent example is the union campaign to get the French national government to take a stake in Alstom – adding to the stake it has recently taken in Peugeot (part of PSA Peugeot Citroën). The latter was done mostly to satisfy workers' unions, rather than consumers wanting to buy more competitively priced cars.

Clientelism can also involve establishing the economic dependence of such special interest groups on government handouts, or by granting favors for individual leaders in these groups, as with board appointments to SOEs, or other perks. For example, profits from state-owned lotteries in many countries are handed out to various special interest groups.

SOEs and other public assets provide excellent opportunities for clientelism. In Brazil, two successive presidents, Luiz Inácio Lula da Silva and Dilma Rousseff, both from the Workers' Party, catered to poorer motorists by leaning on national oil giant Petrobras, to withdraw plans to raise petrol prices in line with world prices. They paid little heed to the losses that private minority shareholders in Petrobras suffered as a result. Brazilian federal police recently raided the home of a former executive at Petrobas, confiscating more than half a million dollars in cash. Prosecutors alleged that corruption affecting Petrobras, including bribes and underhand political donations, cost more than $440 million in inflated contracts. Beyond party politics, however, this highlights the ease with which politicians are able to use state companies as a source of illicit campaign funds. As recently as 2010, Petrobras was a symbol of Brazil's economic rise. Yet, despite massive investments, its production growth has been poor. Returns on capital and its share price have collapsed in the wake of the scandals and falling oil prices.

The Brazilian government also saw to the removal of Roger Agnelli as boss of Vale, the world's biggest miner of iron ore. Although Vale was privatized in 1997, the national Brazilian Development Bank, the BNDES, still owns a large share. The government expressed displeasure at Agnelli's emphasis on exporting iron ore to China instead of building local steel mills.

Musacchio and Lazzarini (2014) analyze Brazilian state-owned assets to demonstrate that loans from BNDES transfer subsidies to large firms without any effect on the stated aims of improved firm-level performance or greater investment. Instead, campaign donations explain BNDES' choice of who receives subsidies. They find that BNDES does not generally pick underperforming projects. Politically connected firms are not necessarily underperformers. Still, the BNDES achieves little, and its function, according to Musacchio and Lazzarini, is merely to move funds to firms that support the right politicians.

Clientelism in SOEs is also prevalent in Italy. Matteo Renzi, Italy's youngest ever prime minister, who came to power in February 2014, announced a few months later that he would change the top executive positions at Enel, Eni, Finmeccanica, and Poste Italiane, the top four companies wholly or partly owned through the Italian Ministry of Economy and Finance. These four firms made up a third of the value of Italy's stock exchange as of summer 2014. In a move seen as a major test of the young prime minister's ability to drive reform, Renzi's immediate, and most eye-catching, decision was to promote three women to chair companies, including steel industry chief executive Emma Marcegaglia at Eni, the oil and gas group. While these women were undoubtedly well qualified, it also illustrates how natural it appeared, even for a reformer, that top positions in SOEs should be used to make political statements.

In many countries clientelism is more subtle. The US electricity industry is dominated by private corporations. However, the federal government owns the huge Tennessee Valley Authority (TVA) and four Power Marketing Administrations (PMAs), which sell power in 33 states. These government power companies have become an anachronism as utility privatization has been pursued across the globe. In his 1996 budget, President Bill Clinton proposed selling off the four PMAs, but this never happened. Leaving the question of privatization aside, turning the TVA and the PMAs into more independent commercially run firms under a holding company would eliminate the clientelism that causes energy overconsumption by allowing these firms to convert their competitive advantage into artificially low power rates. More independence from politics would thus confer an environmental advantage. In addition, it would likely increase efficiency in utility operations.

Conflict of interest

SOEs lobby for their cause, as do many other firms. Often, they are more successful lobbyists than private firms, having easier access to governments and their bureaucracies. They are overseen by, and have regular contacts with, at least some government ministries, and they often have high-level employees or board members that come directly from government, and vice versa. Not least, they are perceived as working for the common good, and their motives may therefore not be scrutinized in the same way as those of representatives from just any private firm.

For example, Don Novey, long-standing president of the California Correctional Peace Officers Association, was a strong lobbyist behind initiatives like the "Three strikes and you're out" law, which led to higher prison populations, a tenfold increase in correctional officers in the state, and increased spending, so that California spends more on its prisons than on higher education. Novey certainly became popular among association members. If Novey had represented employees at private firms or, even worse, investors in private prisons, his campaign would more likely have been perceived as self-serving.

In China, the influence of SOEs on politics is actually claimed to be an advantage. In theory, the management of SOEs, such as China Mobile, is overseen by their primary ownership manager, the State-owned Assets Supervision and Administration Commission. But in practice, these firms have close ties to other departments and, in reality, they are run by the CCP. Management-level employees easily change jobs among these bodies, and this is seen as an important way to build competences among state and party administrators about conditions in various branches.

Yet, the producer perspective can easily entail lobbying that is not only harmful for consumers, but involves a high stakes gamble with the entire economy.

Government wealth can precipitate financial crises

During Vietnam's boom in 2005–10, several well-connected state firms got carried away, borrowing heavily and diversifying without good cause.

In India, state banks have seen more than a tenth of their loan books sour, and they are under political pressure to "extend and pretend" dud loans to crony firms. But a default by Vinashin, a state-owned shipbuilder with an astonishing US$4 billion in accumulated debt, helped spark a banking crisis. Several executives were imprisoned for mismanagement.

China's banking system is not yet liberalized or fully commercial, but is still used to prop up SOEs. Thanks to a government-directed lending boom in 2008–11, banks have accumulated a large share of nonperforming loans. SOEs are often granted easier access to loans and are allowed to live on even when they cannot service their loans. According to Nicholas Lardy, between 2010 and 2012, private firms received, on average, half of the loans going to all enterprises, while producing between two-thirds and three-quarters of China's GDP. With SOEs earning far less than their cost of capital, interest rate liberalization would lead to an increase in credit flowing into the private sector, since they can pay somewhat higher rates and still be profitable.[4]

In each instance, state-owned firms or banks lobbied to convince their owners or bank supervisory authorities to permit laxer regulation. Private banks and firms also lobby, of course, but are rarely allowed the easy mingling of interests that is routine between state-owned firms and government ministries. Some types of lobbying by publicly owned firms can have far-reaching and harmful results.

Take, for example, Fannie Mae (Federal National Mortgage Association) and Freddie Mac (Federal Home Loan Mortgage Corporation) in the US. Both institutions charted a fairly prudential course following their establishment as government-sponsored enterprises (GSEs), a form of quasi-governmental firm. But in 2003 and 2004, they were rocked by a series of accounting scandals that tainted their reputation as well-managed companies. Suddenly, they encountered questions regarding their contribution to lowering mortgage rates, as well as their safety and soundness. Some questioned whether they should be allowed to continue to hold mortgages – by far their most profitable activity – and Senate Republicans moved a bill out of committee that would have prohibited this activity. After that, and perhaps to regain credibility, they markedly stepped up subprime lending, along with lobbying for rules that allowed even more lending.

Managing their political risk required these GSEs to offer congressional members a generous benefits package. Campaign contributions were certainly one element. Between the 2000 and 2008 election cycles, the GSEs, and their employees, contributed more than US$14.6 million to the campaign funds of dozens of senators and house representatives, mostly those on committees important to preserving the GSEs' privileges.[5]

Fannie Mae knew how to take political advantage of its lending, and not just its assets – it often enlisted help from other groups profiting from their activities – the securities industry, homebuilders, and realtors – to sponsor separate fundraising events for the GSEs' key congressional allies. In addition to campaign funds, the GSEs (particularly Fannie Mae) enhanced their power in Congress by setting up "partnership offices" in districts and states of important lawmakers, often hiring relatives of these lawmakers to staff the local offices.

Their lobbying activities were legendary. Between 1998 and 2008, Freddie Mac spent almost US$95 million and Fannie Mae spent almost US$80 million on congressional lobbying. This ranks them 13th and 20th, respectively, among the largest spenders on lobbying fees during that period. Not all of these expenditures were necessary to contact members of Congress, as these GSEs routinely hired lobbyists simply to deprive their opponents of lobbying help. What's more, since lobbyists are frequently part of lawmakers' networks, often including their former staffers, these lobbying expenditures also encouraged members of Congress to support Fannie Mae and Freddie Mac as a means of supplementing the income of their friends.

Other credit crises share this element of lobbying by publicly (as well as privately) owned firms. The earlier savings and loan (S&L) crisis in the US that culminated in the 1980s is one of the largest financial scandals before 2000. Close to one-third (more than 1,000 out of 3,234) of S&L banks in the country went bankrupt between 1986 and 1995. These S&Ls (also known as thrifts) were not formally state owned, but in practice many were intertwined with local politicians in various roles, or even completely controlled by local politicians. One example is the Lincoln Savings and Loan Association scandal. Here, five US senators, known as the "Keating Five," were implicated in an influence-peddling scheme named after Charles Keating, the politically well-connected owner of Lincoln Savings (through his real estate firm). In this particular instance, he donated up to $1.4 million in contributions to these senators in the late 1980s, who then intervened in a federal regulatory investigation of the bank.

In another example, Silverado Savings and Loan collapsed in 1988 at a cost to taxpayers of $1.3 billion. Neil Bush, son of then US Vice President George H.W. Bush, was on the board of directors of Silverado at the time. The US Office of Thrift Supervision investigated Silverado's failure and found that Neil Bush had engaged in numerous "breaches of his fiduciary duties involving multiple conflicts of interest." As a director of a failing thrift, Bush voted to approve $100 million in what were ultimately bad loans to two of his business partners.

A similar development brought Spain to the brink of bankruptcy during the recent financial crisis. Spanish regional banks were not always formally government owned. More often, they were owned by foundations, but in practice worked in liaison with local politicians on their boards who encouraged lavish lending to local development projects. When the housing bubble burst, these banks went bust in droves. Spain's large private banks were forced to absorb many of them and as a result suffered severe difficulties themselves.

Even in well-run Germany, regional government-owned banks have been a disaster. The following example is in no way extreme, but rather it is a story that, in different ways, was repeated many times over. In 2007, the Bayrische Landesbank (BayernLB), a federal state bank owned by the taxpayers of Bavaria, was happy to risk its citizens' money by purchasing a bank in a different country altogether, buying the Austrian bank Hypo Alpe Adria for €1.6 billion. In turn, this bank was intended to expand into Eastern Europe. BayernLB had already lost a bidding battle for the Vienna-based BAWAG PSK bank, leading to speculation that this was why it was in such a hurry to acquire Hypo Alpe Adria. Only two years later, its hubris ended in tears when the Austrian state was forced to take over Hypo Alpe Adria to avoid it entering bankruptcy. The loss to Bavarian taxpayers totaled €3.7 billion.

When BayernLB acquired Hypo, its supervisory board included several local politicians. The superior administrative board comprised four senior Bavarian state governmental politicians under Edmund Stoiber, the then minister-president of the state of Bavaria and former chairman of the Christian Social Union. Other senior state officials included Kurt Falthauser (minister of finance), Erwin Huber (minister of economics), Günter Beckstein (minister of the interior), and Georg Schmid (secretary of state in the ministry of the interior).[6] Despite the importance of this acquisition and the impact it had on the main financial institutions within Bavaria, of the six meetings dealing with the Hypo Alpe Adria acquisition, Huber and Beckstein attended none and Schmid only one, according to the press covering the case.

The contract signed between Hypo Alpe Adria and BayernLB ended in a series of investigation committees, prosecutions, criminal proceedings, and civil cases. Seven former members of the supervisory board were put on trial in early 2014. This included Wilhelm Schmidt, the former CEO and chairman, and his replacement, Michael Kemmer. They are accused of having flouted risks and having paid too high a price.

Our main point here is not to highlight the almost farcical mismanagement of a state-owned bank. Rather, we want to illustrate how the controlling boards of these banks all too often are filled with the same people who, in their government roles, must participate in decisions regarding economic policy and bank regulation, creating an inescapable conflict of interest between government as the regulator and government as an owner. The intertwined roles that government officials and politicians often have would rarely be allowed in relation to private firms.

These examples show how owning wealth in the name of the public can expose a country's democratic processes and economic policies to grave danger in subtle ways.

Neglecting the consumer perspective

Even more subtle, but nonetheless corrosive effects arise in countries with an extensive state-owned sector. These stem from the way politicians are forced to assume a dual responsibility: first, for defining demand for and financing provision of public services, and second, for delivering the production of those services through publicly owned firms. This creates an obvious conflict of interest. Government "for the people" should, by definition, be on the side of the consumer. Its job is to protect consumer and public interests. This job does not square easily with a government that knows it will be held accountable as a manager of an SOE if their firm fails to deliver.

A natural, although likely misguided choice politicians make is to govern their SOEs through public directives, board representation, or by appointing party members to managerial posts in the hope of forcing the enterprise to meet voters' demands. Paradoxically, this strategy often has the opposite effect. Political leaders who put themselves in charge of SOEs also assume responsibility in the eyes of their voters who then blame the politicians if things go wrong. As a result, politicians easily lose interest in formulating consumer demands or making SOE performance more transparent. Such measures only raise the risk that poor management will be exposed, and the blame will fall squarely on the governing politicians.

For example, state-owned airlines such as Air France or Lufthansa had little intention of offering low-cost flights until private competitors forced their hand. Successive governments in France and Germany had, as owners of these airlines, little regard for the customer. Instead, they focused on international expansion. And they caved in to unions and ended up paying exorbitant remuneration packages to pilots and other employees. The extent of this consumer loss is now being exposed by the budget airlines that are mushrooming across the world, such as Norwegian, Europe's third-largest budget airline. This small upstart only got going as a low-cost carrier after 2002 but manages much more efficiently than its competitor, the state-owned SAS. While SAS still struggles through consecutive restructuring plans and seems unable to reach profitability, Norwegian has been profitable since 2006. It is now expanding outside Europe, offering routes to almost every corner of the world. Rivals, trade unions such as AFL-CIO, the largest federation of trade unions in the US, and some US politicians accuse Norwegian of social dumping and are lobbying Washington to prevent Norwegian from obtaining a license for its Ireland-registered long-haul subsidiary, Norwegian Air International. In the meantime, consumers show their appreciation for their services in growing numbers.

Proponents of public ownership often express fears over the overexploitation of land or other assets when these are held in, or sold into, private hands.

In many cases, however, it works the other way around. Many African countries have discovered that wildlife is better protected on private concessions than in public national parks. A perhaps extreme example of the mechanisms leading to overexploitation of public lands in the US is the incident involving Cliven Bundy, a Nevada cattle rancher, and his so-called "Patriot Party." Bundy has refused to pay or even apply for grazing permits on federally owned land in the state of Nevada. When officials from the federal Bureau of Land Management, along with contractors and supported by law enforcement representatives, attempted to enforce several court orders (after 20 years of court actions) by confiscating cattle on public land, they were confronted by over 1,000 supporters Bundy had called on, many armed and wearing military fatigues. Bundy rallied his anti-government supporters to stare down the government representatives.

The agents were seeking to enforce a court ruling that Bundy should remove his 900-odd cattle from the federal land on which they grazed. His private supporters brought an awesome armory with them. After a brief, tense stand-off, during which the protesters trained assault rifles on their perceived adversaries, the officials released the 400-odd cattle they had rounded up and beat a retreat. Bundy and his supporters are dismissed as extremists, but among the supporters were various legislators such as Dean Heller, Nevada's Republican senator.

While this incident may have been unusually colorful, it illustrates the political pressures that many times cause federal land to be unprotected land. Entitlements to use federal land are rarely revoked. It hardly helps that the Bureau of Land Management is a bureaucratic nightmare. Apart from excessive red tape, many types of subsidies (running to hundreds of millions annually) not only cheat taxpayers, but actually encourage overgrazing.

Similarly, Francis Fukuyama gives a striking description of how the US Forest Service decayed from being a fairly independent and highly professional warden of national forests.[7] Today, it appears to be a rather bloated, dysfunctional bureaucracy, operating under a multitude of often contradictory mandates from Congress and the courts.

Having described the nefarious side effects that poor institutions that govern public wealth can have, the next question is how large public wealth actually is, and how it might contribute much more to countries' internal development. This is discussed in Chapter 4.

4

The size and potential of public wealth

Previous chapters looked at the detrimental effects that extensive public commercial assets can have on governance, GDP growth, and democracy. Yet public wealth comprises much more than state-owned companies. In fact, SOEs and financial institutions constitute the smallest part of the government portfolio, be it at the central government level or the regional and local level. The largest segment of public commercial assets is real estate: property and land with an economic value that often does not appear on any balance sheet.

On top of that, but outside our attempts to value public assets, is infrastructure – roads, bridges, and railroads – financed through the state budget for which no market may exist, but which could be run in ways that better promote growth and development – as well as national parks and other assets held by quasi-governmental organizations and run by politicians in governmental positions.

How much public wealth is there and can it be put to better use? What alternatives do countries have? The cover story for *The Economist* on January 11, 2014 was – "The $9 Trillion Sale."[1] The article highlights the size of public commercial assets and urges immediate privatization of much of them to stimulate growth and restore public financial health.

The last quarter of a century has been rife with violent and always ideological discussions of state ownership versus privatization. We call this a "phony war." The polarized debate has detraction attention from the most important issue, the quality of asset governance. For any ownership mode, be it private, public, mutual or cooperative, there is a wide range of alternative management models/styles. Making the right choices will have a major impact on performance and value to the ultimate owners in their role as taxpayers as well as to consumers. It is time to focus on all the profit that is being left on the table to be captured by vested interests, after all the arguments over who owns the table.

In this chapter, we discuss the current value, and the untapped future potential, that is locked in to state-owned assets. Later chapters focus on reforming public wealth and providing better governance for it.

The elusive quest of assessing value

Governments worldwide have only a patchy idea of the national wealth under their control, as many of these assets are hidden. Poor accounting standards, unclear and poorly defined economic statistics and the lack of a consolidated asset list are part of the problem. Accounts are mostly maintained by central national governments and somewhat arbitrarily labeled, as in "financial" versus "nonfinancial" assets.

Information on publicly owned real estate assets is often stuck somewhere between a formal cadastral survey and disorderly land registries, and sometimes kept by users or managers in different ministerial departments, due to inconsistent legislation. Attempts to centralize information has even met with resistance, where some departments refuse to deliver documentation they have on file or under management, seemingly due to staff fears of losing authority.[2]

Few governments, however, face challenges as overwhelming as the Greek government, which lacks a proper land registry. Despite having received more than US$100 million in EU aid over the past two decades in order to establish a national land registry, less than 7% of the country has been properly mapped.[3] The majority of assets in the government portfolio also lack proper documentation, covering everything from simple clear title, to registration, zoning, and licensing issues.

The biggest challenge in valuing public wealth in many countries remains with real estate, where records are often fragmented and scattered among several departments, each holding on to their piece of the puzzle, denying others access to their information. Any attempt to assess value, budgeting for asset management activities, and evaluating public asset portfolio performance gets lost in procrastination and bureaucracy. As a result, assets are managed on an ad hoc, often reactive basis.[4]

The use of better accounting or budgeting methodologies alone does not automatically guarantee better use of these assets. Professional and consolidated organization is also necessary with the intention of governing the assets to create value. The current institutional design in many countries begs the question: "Is the government even interested in a more efficient governance?" Consider the US, where many local governments have budgeting, accounting, and asset management units as three different branches with little interaction.

Policy analyses and statistics often focus entirely on the financial assets held by central governments and the more visible, listed SOEs. Few attempts to value nonfinancial assets such as real estate have been made at this time. Moreover, as with icebergs, assets at lower levels, in local and regional governments, or more anonymously, land and property, are rarely included in the available information. The question to ask here is how much any country's balance sheet would improve if these assets were valued (whether correctly or at all) and made more transparent. Still, this is a difficult exercise, and one which most governments shy away from.

The primary conceptual problem is that the value of state property depends entirely on how well it is managed. A nationalized company, operating at a low level of profitability that can therefore only replace depreciated capital, has no value at all in a balance sheet where assets are recorded at market value. But with only a small improvement in management efficiency, a slight lift in profitability engenders a stream of expected returns, and thus, potentially, also significantly increases present value.

This conceptual problem with determining the true value of property is especially relevant when considering government-owned land, as this is used without accounting for the opportunity cost of the land. Militaries around the world, for example, often use buildings and land with potentially high market value for purposes that could easily be located on less valuable property. Recent examples are the various barracks in central London, such as the Chelsea Barracks in one of London's most expensive residential areas, which was only recently sold in order to be developed by Qatari Diar and the CPC Group.

In many cases, these underutilized public assets are simply treated as if their value were zero. As an example, the US Department of the Interior oversees approximately 260 million acres (105 million hectares), mainly through the Bureau of Land Management. The largest known source of oil shale in the world is the Green River Formation in the US states of Colorado, Utah, and Wyoming. But this happens to be mostly on (under) federal and state land. The shale gas and oil revolution in the US has taken place almost entirely on private land. Whether a patch of land has an oil well on it or not makes a big difference to its value.

These examples also illustrate our claim that better management of public assets can render large capital gains for the state. A small increase in annual return produces a large increase in present value. Still, valuation of public assets must be based on current yield, not on a pie-in-the-sky estimate. The countries that have made some headway conservatively use a mix of historic costs, market value, and replacement cost to estimate public wealth. Even so, the sums are overwhelming.

How large is public wealth?

In Chapter 2, we noted the OECD's estimates for the value of SOEs. But those constitute only one segment of public wealth. The larger portion of public wealth consists of fixed assets, including property and land, much of which is held by local governments.

For example, it is estimated that of the 3.9 billion hectares of the world's forests, 86% are publicly owned. This includes approximately 200 million hectares of tribal and community-managed forests. In Russia, 100% of forests are publicly owned, with public ownership dominating in the other 11 states in the Commonwealth of Independent States and several other former communist countries. In Western Europe, the percentages of publicly owned forest lands are 54% in Germany, 77% in Greece, 66% in Ireland, and 68% in Switzerland. In the US, somewhat more forest land is under private ownership, with private owners together accounting for 57% of forest ownership.

The US Bureau of Economic Analysis calculates that the value of nonfinancial public assets in the US, as a whole, amounted to 74% of GDP in 2011.[5] Of this, the federal share of these nonfinancial assets has been shrinking, now amounting to less than 20% of GDP. The lion's share of these assets are owned by states and municipalities.

The UK, along with New Zealand and Sweden, is one of the few countries that produces a national balance sheet of its public assets. The UK version, the National Balance Sheet, aggregated by the Office of National Statistics, estimated in 2012 that the net worth of financial and nonfinancial assets of the general government was a negative £259 billion, due to government debt, of which central government was a negative £763 billion and local government a positive £504 billion.[6]

The good news is that the UK makes a strong effort to produce a comprehensive picture of public assets. However, the picture is still rather fragmented and the valuation of assets would most likely never have passed accountancy standards in a private sector company managing these kind of assets. It is based on the Whole of Government Accounts (WGA), an initiative by HM Treasury to consolidate the audited accounts of around 4,000 organizations across the public sector in order to produce a comprehensive, accounts-based picture of the financial position of the UK public sector. WGA is based on International Financial Reporting Standards, the system of accounts used internationally by the private sector. The accounts are independently audited by the comptroller and auditor general, and at the end of 2013, put the value of the government's total assets at £1,264 billion (US$1,987 billion), comprising £747 billion of land, buildings, dwellings, infrastructure, and other property, plant and equipment; and £516 billion of trade and other receivables, loans and deposits with banks, and other assets. This value would correspond to around 70% of GDP.[7]

The WGA also tallies total liability of £2,893 billion, while the net liability (net equity) in WGA terms is £1,630 billion. Some argue that this means the government would be broke if seen as a private enterprise either using the National Balance Sheet or the WGA. But this gives a lopsided impression, since the government can also count on future tax revenue (which is not counted as current assets) to cover future pension liabilities.

An earlier initiative by HM Treasury in 2007 produced the National Asset Register (NAR) of all central government-owned assets, by questioning all departments. This survey mapped out all tangible fixed assets (including military and heritage assets), intangible fixed assets (such as software licenses), and fixed asset investments (such as shareholdings) owned by departments, but excluding current assets. The NAR calculated that the net book value of all central government-owned assets in the UK in 2007 was £337 billion (US$530 billion).[8]

In addition, the Audit Commission expects to publish in March 2015, as enabled by the Local Audit and Accountability Act 2014, what it calls "value for money profiles," which bring together publicly available data about the cost, performance, and activity of local councils and fire authorities. The value of a council's estate it is using for this exercise as recorded in council accounts is called the net book value (NBV). It records the value of an asset to the council, taking depreciation into account. In 2012/13, the total NBV for all English councils was £170 billion.[9] Figure 4.1 compares these four valuations of UK public wealth.

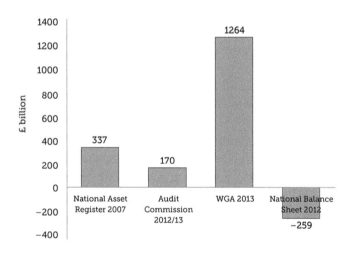

FIGURE 4.1 Valuations of UK public wealth along four overlapping tracks

Nevertheless, given the lack of a central cadaster or real estate register, the question remains: Has the government has been able to capture all government-owned assets, be they central, local or regional? Furthermore, if the data is not centralized and consolidated under a single management with a unified objective, is it coherent enough to be able to assess a potential market value?

The numbers provided by the Audit Commission comprise only local council assets and are limited geographically to England. The NAR contains only central government assets valued using their NBV as at March 31, 2005, allowing a comparison to be drawn between the information in the NAR and that published in government resource accounts. Acquisitions and disposals of assets are valued using their NBV at the time of the acquisition or disposal of only those assets worth more than £1 million. Therefore, the real value of assets is almost certainly underestimated when they were acquired a long time ago or for a lower amount, but still carrying a substantial market value.

It is likely that even the NBV of UK public commercial assets owned by the central government exceeds all the above estimates if properly consolidated and accounted for. The market value of all assets owned by the central government would probably be closer to the equivalent of national GDP, with the commercial assets owned at the local level as a multiple of the central government portfolio.

The good news is that with this drive for better transparency, central government and local councils in the UK are looking at new solutions in their approach to asset management. Long-term leases or partnerships with private sector specialists and community groups, for example, allow councils to reconfigure the public estate while still retaining public ownership.[10] Other initiatives, such as in Kent, help local public service providers to work together, owning fewer but higher quality buildings, which are more intensively used, at less cost.[11]

Although the UK is probably one of the most, if not the most, transparent country in the world in terms of its public sector real estate, as we can see above, the various valuation efforts and the many different results do not compare well with what is required in the private sector and what would be required to efficiently manage such a portfolio. A proper national balance sheet consolidating all assets in a coherent way is still very much in demand, as suggested by Buiter as long ago as 1983.[12] The lack of a full inventory of real estate assets and the different valuation techniques applied to different kinds of public sector assets do not allow for proper market values to be assigned to each of these assets. This prevents the government from forming a coherent strategy and applying an opportunity cost to the use of these assets. Decades of efforts reinventing the wheel by coming up with public sector instruments and public sector organizations that could mimic the private sector have mostly failed.

Worldwide public wealth

The International Monetary Fund (IMF) has done the most so far to aggregate individual country data on public assets.[13] Even so, it has only done this for 27 countries. Cross-country comparisons are still precarious, and all estimates tend to err on the low side.

Countries report mostly financial assets (in the IMF definition, this also includes stocks in SOEs) and nonfinancial assets that consist partly of so-called "produced assets." These include fixed assets (buildings, machinery, and equipment), inventories, intellectual property, and valuables like artwork, precious metals, and jewelry.

Fewer countries register data on "nonproduced" assets such as natural resources – oil, gas or minerals, contracts, and leases.[14] Nonproduced assets could potentially be an important source of wealth and revenue for governments, as they are, for example, in Australia (nearly 69% of GDP), Costa Rica (48% of GDP), and Japan (26% of GDP). Most importantly, the extent to which local and regional public assets are included differs between countries and is generally incomplete.

Even with these caveats, the results of this exercise are revealing. Despite nonfinancial assets likely to be underestimated, they usually exceed financial assets. Even more remarkable is that the sum of financial and nonfinancial assets in nearly all countries exceeds gross public debt, including the well-known high debt countries like France, Germany, Japan, and the UK. For the US, assets and debts are roughly on par.

Figure 4.2 shows the results for the countries the IMF valued, with some additional countries, such as Sweden, Ukraine, Latvia, Lithuania, Slovenia, and Israel, that the authors have assessed. (Local and regional public assets and nonfinancial assets are only partially included.) It is important

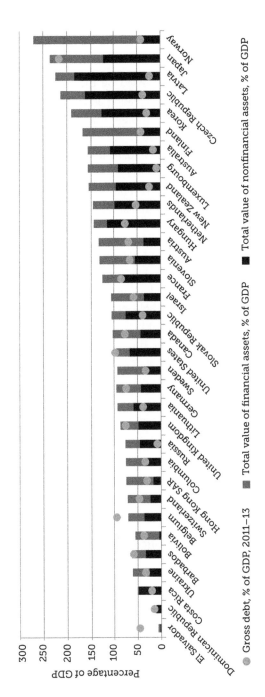

FIGURE 4.2 General government assets and liabilities, as a percentage of GDP

Sources: IMF (2013); authors

to remember that these countries are simply the ones that keep the best statistics, not necessarily those with the largest public assets. China, for example, is not included.

On average, across the 27 countries assessed by the IMF, public assets amount to 114% of GDP. Even when calculating an average weighted by the size of GDP, government assets are still larger than GDP. The additional countries we valued confirm this estimate.[15] A naive extrapolation from these countries to the world as a whole implies that global public assets exceed both total public debt (US$54 trillion) and total global GDP (US$75 trillion). We also extrapolated in more sophisticated ways that take account of country differences with similar results.[16]

The values included in official databases for central government are generally underestimated due to problems with accounting standards and the lack of a consolidated list of public assets. Local government assets and natural resources are not included or are only partially included. On average, subnational governments hold more than one-half of total nonfinancial assets. For the countries that have included local government values, the share tends to be even higher. This indicates that if all countries had comprehensively included the local levels, the total public assets recorded would be substantially higher.

In sum, we argue that it is safe to assume that the aggregate value of assets held at the central government level worldwide is at least equal to global GDP – US$75 trillion. In fact, it is almost certain that this estimate is well on the low end. At the very least, this should spur every level of all governments to make a considerable effort to gain a better understanding of the wealth they sit on.

Asset management and public commercial assets in a global perspective

There is also a financial side to public commercial asset management. Let us compare how private and public assets are managed. The global total of assets held by pension funds, sovereign wealth funds (SWF), insurance companies, mass affluent, and high-net-worth individuals (HNWI) amounted to about US$180 trillion at the end of 2013. Of that, around 36% is managed by external professional managers through the asset management industry.[17]

If we thought of governments and central banks[18] as people's "wealth managers," then we could draw up a comparison, as in Figure 4.3. Governments clearly appear to be the largest wealth managers of any category.

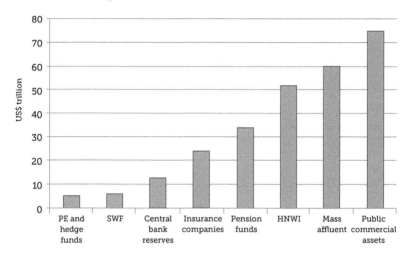

FIGURE 4.3 Governments are the largest wealth managers: assets under external management in different categories

Sources: PwC (2013); World Bank; authors' calculations

The government itself outsources only minute volumes to external asset managers. If we instead ask how much of public assets is managed by professional managers in national wealth funds, the answer is that only US$1 trillion (or less than 1.5%) are managed in an external professional setting.[19] Thus, public assets is the segment least managed by external professional managers.

Another way of looking at this is to view all wealth as ultimately owned by citizens. Wealth ostensibly owned by private firms is reflected in the value of their shares, which, in the end, is also owned by private citizens. In Figure 4.4, total global wealth (net of debts) is shown as the sum of household assets and public assets.[20]

After these attempts to quantify the value of public assets, what import do higher returns on these assets have for their owners, the citizens?

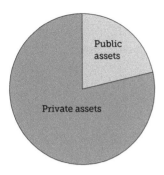

FIGURE 4.4 World wealth divided into public and private assets
Sources: Credit Suisse (2014); authors

How does a higher return on public wealth affect the economy?

The implication we draw from public commercial assets being at least equal to GDP is that if, through better management, the rate of return on public assets is raised by only 1%, this would correspond to 1% of total GDP each year. Raising the rate of return by 2% would roughly equal world spending on R&D, while a 3.5% increase in returns would equal all global spending on basic infrastructure – transport, energy, water, and communication. But where do these hidden resources come from and what is the macroeconomic implication of higher returns on public wealth? This can be confusing, and worth spelling out exactly.

A starting point can be two thought experiments. First, suppose that a country's public wealth consists entirely of cash in the bank. Under current conditions, the interest rate is low and hardly likely to rise much. A higher rate of return on public wealth is unlikely.

Alternatively, suppose that public wealth is entirely invested in productive capital, for machinery and buildings in a state-owned factory. Then, a 3.5% higher rate of return on public wealth – all else being equal and assuming that public wealth is equal to GDP – will translate into a GDP that is 3.5% higher. Note that this does not mean that the growth rate of GDP is 3.5 percentage points higher, which would have to be deemed improbably high. If some of the yield is invested, there can be more lasting effects on the growth rate. But if the extra yield on public wealth is consumed, the only effect will be that GDP stabilizes at a level 3.5% higher than it would have been if the yield on public assets had remained lower.

Is that achievable? In fact, there is a sizeable research literature indicating that public investments can have an important effect on GDP levels and growth,[21] and in later chapters we will show in more detail how the returns on such public investments can vary significantly depending on how well they are invested. Our conclusion from such comparisons is that a 3.5% higher rate of return on public productive investments is not at all unrealistic. For example, the average return on assets for state entities in China has been around 4.6% since 2008, compared with 9.1% for private companies.[22]

The rate of return on public wealth, however, also depends on how the value of publicly owned assets changes, independent of actual investments made. For example, if the state of Massachusetts moved the Boston Logan airport from prime waterfront land to cheaper land inland, it would stand to make a large windfall gain in real estate assets on the waterfront land that would probably well exceed the cost of moving the airport. Indirectly, GDP would also be affected due to ensuing investments and growth prospects. Living standards might rise since people appreciate waterfront views. But mainly it would represent a gain in wealth for the state, which could then be used, for example, for greatly needed infrastructure spending.

Capturing these elements, better governance of public wealth can raise returns in four ways that have different macroeconomic implications:

1 *Better management of liquid financial holdings:* higher returns provide more public revenue, without necessarily increasing GDP. We largely neglect this in our book, but it is an obvious strategy that should be pursued.
2 *Better management of SOEs:* raises the productivity of public investments, which raises GDP, but can also improve the valuation of SOEs based on expectations of future performance. For example, Norway's Statoil is valued much higher than Russia's Gazprom.[23]
3 *Better management of public real estate and infrastructure:*
   – can raise productivity of state investments and thus raise GDP
   – can yield social values such as shorter travel times due to smarter infrastructure investment, which can raise GDP and living standards in ways that are not measured in GDP

– produces capital gains as the valuation of real estate increases.

4 *Higher and more accurate valuation of public assets:* can lower the risk premium attached to a country's debt. This lowers public expenses directly, but may also lower interest rate costs to banks and other large firms. We largely ignore this aspect in our book.

In later sections, we will show that increased rates of returns on public wealth of a few percentage points through these channels should be quite achievable outcomes of better management. But first, a closer look at Ukraine, which provides an illustrative example of a country close to bankruptcy but with huge public wealth that is poorly governed.

Example: Ukraine

Oligarchs have dominated Ukraine since its independence in 1991. During the early 1990s, vast amounts of public assets previously held in the communist system were transferred at bargain prices to well-connected cronies. Although the country continues to score among the highest on *The Economist* crony-capitalism index,[24] the remaining portfolio of public commercial assets nevertheless represents a significant share of Ukraine's economy, and plays a dominant role in the economy through the transport, utilities, energy, and real estate sectors.

The portfolio of enterprises constitutes both an opportunity as well as a considerable fiscal risk for the government. Opportunities include the potential benefits of restructuring, liberalization, and possible dividends from the portfolio. But risks involve the need to provide fiscal support and other transfers of budgetary resources, including issuing guarantees for enterprise debt and facilitating lines of credit.

The portfolio of commercial assets includes corporates, financial institutions, and more than 3,500 entities owned by central government, as fully state-owned institutions, although a large part of these are not active entities and numbers do not include real estate assets.[25] These include two of the largest banks in Ukraine, the State Export-Import Bank of Ukraine (Ukreximbank) and the State Savings Bank of Ukraine (Oschadbank).

The total value of the Ukrainian portfolio of public commercial assets most likely exceeds current conservative estimates of US$70 billion, or some 60% of GDP. Ukraine's Naftogaz alone would represent a large share of this value, as the energy sector is being liberalized and the company accordingly broken up into transportation, storage, distribution, and extraction. Moreover, the property component of the country's portfolio is entirely unaccounted for and largely unknown, but includes much of the country's commercial property and all forestry assets.

Public assets at the national level have a negative fiscal impact, with losses amounting to a net cost to the country in 2013 of over 11.8% of GDP in total.[26] At the same time, privatization receipts have stalled, falling to less than 0.2% of GDP in the same year. Added to this, public guarantees issued for SOE debt, totaling 8.4% of GDP (as of May 2014), for which nearly 77% are foreign exchange denominated guarantees, expose government finances to significant exchange rate risk.[27]

The fiscal and economic risks for Ukraine are exacerbated by geopolitical factors, including a planned fourth pipeline – South Stream – between Russia and Europe across the Black Sea. Although currently on hold, if it were revived, the increase in transportation capacity between Russian and Western Europe would reduce the importance of Naftogaz and the value of its transportation and storage assets to a fraction of its current potential value. Adding to this, many vital state-owned industries are located in the eastern parts of the country currently enduring fighting between Ukrainian forces and pro-Russian separatists and allegedly Russian-backed military forces (as of February 2015). The outcome of this conflict will significantly impact the public asset portfolio and thereby government finances, as well as economic growth in Ukraine.

Naftogaz

Naftogaz is the central government-owned and vertically integrated oil and gas company. It is the largest company in Ukraine, of huge strategic importance to the country in economic, political, and even security terms. It has a wide range of conflicting objectives, functions, and reporting lines. It is nominally a commercial company, but it lacks legal title to the assets it is established to operate – all of which remain under direct ownership of the state.

Historically, it has appointed government officials to its board, while management reports directly to the Cabinet and the Ministry of Fuel and Energy on regulatory and operational issues. Subsidies through Naftogaz provided to households in the form of underpriced gas and heating costs nearly 5% of GDP per year. The domestic business model of Naftogaz is entirely dependent on substantial government subsidies throughout its entire value chain. This system of subsidies notably weighs heavily on national finances, while it promotes energy overconsumption, discourages investment in delivery systems, and erodes incentives to increase domestic production. With the significant budgetary constraints the country currently faces, these untargeted implicit gas subsidies also divert resources away from more focused social and infrastructure spending.[28]

A state audit report in 2009 concluded that the company's operations were nontransparent, and that information on its financial performance and foreign trade activities was contradictory and confusing. The Ministry of Fuel and Energy does not have a specific mandate to perform oversight and control over the company's activities, and it also lacks the analytical capacity to do this in any real sense. At the same time, the company's internal audit committee has been denied access to financial information, despite significant overruns to the financial plan, misappropriations totaling US$468 million from the company budget, significant growth in wage arrears and bad loans, as well as large amounts in the company's budget that goes to "sponsorship and charity."[29] To address these challenges, the government has initiated an effort to establish a more commercial-oriented energy market, with fair tariffs and the unbundling of the company, to ensure operational sustainability and business value, in accordance with the EU's Third Energy Package.

Ukraine has one of the highest energy intensities in Europe, with energy use per unit of GDP 10 times above the OECD average. This hampers modernization throughout the country's entire industrial complex. It has also maintained extremely low prices on sales of gas to households and district heating companies, preventing any change to its market practices.

Consolidating ownership and instituting independent, professional management of the portfolio of public commercial assets would no doubt provide a huge boost to democracy and the development of the economy in Ukraine. Government ownership of commercial assets brings with it a number of conflicting roles and objectives, which, if separated and professionally managed with a comprehensive ownership approach, would considerably improve development for the country. But, for this, the current complex web of overlapping and sometimes contradictory legislation would need to be completely reworked. The professional management of public assets requires the support of strong state institutions and a vibrant civil society, and, in return, this would also help provide a much firmer base for a sounder democracy where interest group lobbying for the spoils from public wealth loses some of its raison d'être.

Achieving higher returns for public assets

What is the evidence that better management of public assets can achieve considerably higher returns and even GDP growth? Several studies show how the quality of institutions makes a big difference to the extent to which public capital contributes to a country's productivity growth.[30] One particularly interesting study examined the productivity of public investment in low-income countries.[31] This study used the Public Investment Management Index (PIMI), composed of 17 indicators grouped into four stages of the public investment management cycle: project appraisal, project selection, project implementation, and project evaluation. After estimating the effect of PIMI-adjusted public capital on GDP growth, the authors concluded that, on average, public capital in these low-income countries loses about half its value due to mismanagement, with large variations between countries, depending on the quality of management of public capital.

Later chapters will delve deeper into how active ownership of assets can raise the returns to SOEs. But how can better management improve the use and valuation of other public assets?

A large share of these assets consists of real estate. Private companies often have a clear understanding that the value of good property management is vital to their businesses and see it as an integrated part of their business operations. For large companies, this has led to a variety of business and ownership models, mainly with the aim of consolidating their property portfolio by vesting their assets into a separate holding company, to allow for a better and more integrated strategy based on the highest possible transparency and more efficient management. More efficient utilization of space and property development and synergies of procurement of services, including electricity/heating, waste management, as well as cleaning and maintenance services, make a big difference.

Depending on the financial situation and the operational linkage between the properties and the actual business, different governance methods and ownership models have been applied, ranging from hiring professionals to outsourcing governance on a contractual basis in order to develop the value of the portfolio. Subsequently, ownership could take any form from full ownership to inviting a strategic/financial partner or an IPO, even a complete divestiture of the portfolio – once fully developed.

As an example, Time Warner, one of New York City's largest commercial tenants, is looking to consolidate most of its four million square feet of office space. It would like to move to a less expensive part of Manhattan, and vacate the Time Warner Center, the Time & Life building at Rockefeller Center, and many of its other 13 buildings. The company estimated that cutting back on its real estate footprint could save as much as $150 million a year.[32]

In Belgium, an unusual initiative to reduce real estate needs was taken by Frank Van Massenhove, president of the Belgian Federal Service Social Security since 2002. Van Massenhove was awarded the title Public Manager of the Year in 2007 after turning a bureaucratic dinosaur into a modern, flexible, and attractive work environment. A key to this was allowing employees to work from home. It turned out that nearly 92% of them could do their jobs just as easily from their own home. Allowing more of this work at home enabled a significant cutback in the amount of office space needed.

This strategy also proved successful for the Swedish government, who decided to vest its real estate assets in several segmented holding companies. As an example, the portfolio of Akademiska Hus, the specialist real estate manager of university properties, increased in value from an initial SEK 7 billion to more than SEK 64 billion over 20 years, partly through more professional management and development.[33] And by leasing out some 140 million square feet of property, returning rents have increased 36% from 1998 to 2008, compared to a consumer price index increase of 17%.

Finland pursued a more consolidated strategy, and in 1999 placed much of its central government-owned real estate into a single holding company – Senate Properties. It now manages some 10,000 government properties, consisting of over 65 million square feet of rented floor space, and could serve as a successful example of a consolidated holding company of government real estate. Senate Properties works as a fully commercial entity and yields a 4% return on shareholders' equity and a 19% profit margin.[34] The business is divided into four main operating segments: ministries and special premises, offices, defense and security, and real estate development and sales.

In 2011, Greece formally placed the management of central government-owned real estate into ETAD, a common holding company, but has so far failed to manage its property well.[35] Despite more than 30 years' effort, this new company and its predecessors have not been able to create a clear record of the state's holdings and their permitted uses, or more generally produce the sort of information that a prudent manager of real estate would need to administer the affairs of the property portfolio properly and for the benefit of the owner. Furthermore, more than one year after the merger and the establishment of ETAD as a new company, it still has not published its constitutional documents. This illustrates that vesting all the assets into a holding company is not enough without establishing proper governance, transparency, and hiring and properly incentivizing professional managers.

Similarly, in the US, the General Service Administration is tasked with centralizing service purchasing and transparency without having the proper tools or mandate to manage the properties professionally. Instead, property ownership and management are decentralized among the various federal government agencies, holding in total around 1.1 million buildings, of which 79% are used by the federal government and with a total operating cost of US$30 billion annually. This led to a congressional bill in 2012 requiring the government to sell or redevelop high-value properties, consolidating space, and disposing of unneeded assets.[36] According to the Office of Management and Budget, such a process could generate $15 billion in revenue from property sales within the next 10 years; additional savings would come from reduced federal spending on leases, energy, and maintenance.[37]

Making public wealth productive

The fact that public wealth exceeds gross debt in most countries shows that most countries are richer than they understand. Yet, this is hardly a license to spend more. Wealth is an asset only if it is put to good use.

Privatization can sometimes be the best way to make public assets more productive. But a country experiencing difficulty managing its public assets is, in many cases, not in a good position to properly carry out a privatization and will generally have equal difficulty maintaining effective regulation afterward. Many countries also face political restrictions, not least a worry that the proceeds from privatization will not be spent wisely or that assets will not be sold at the maximum price. A political structure that mismanages SOEs may not succeed very well with privatization either. Instead, in Chapter 10, we will argue for more independent management of public assets, such as through a national wealth fund, which also develops these assets into the best position to be sold into the private sector at some future date while still maximizing value.

Much can be achieved even in the absence of an outright public asset fire sale. Many measures to maximize the value of the public portfolio and minimize risk also improve credibility to all stakeholders, including domestic and international investors.

In Chapter 5, we describe how politicians can reinvent their role to truly represent citizens, rather than trying to be capitalists.

5

Politicians as consumer advocates instead of quasi-capitalists

Most would agree that the public wealth could be managed better. This book, however, makes a much more far-reaching claim. Better institutions to govern public wealth can improve democracy and make it easier for politicians and administrators to represent their citizens rather than succumb to pressure from all those striving to share in the spoils of public wealth. In this chapter, we will illustrate how public monopolies can potentially give consumers much better services, if politics was more concerned with citizen welfare and less with protecting SOEs. This also requires that SOEs must be regulated on a par with private firms. One illustration is the way airports, airlines, and traffic control are handled in many countries.

Airports and airlines

Airports and airlines used to be regarded as a vital part of transport infrastructure. Nearly all major US airports are owned by state and local governments, with the federal government subsidizing airport renovation and expansion. By contrast, airports have been fully or partly privatized in many foreign cities, including Athens, Auckland, Brussels, Copenhagen, Frankfurt, London, Melbourne, Naples, Rome, Sydney, and Vienna. Britain led the way with the 1987 privatization of the British Airports Authority, which owns Heathrow and other airports. To proceed with reforms in the

US, Congress should take the lead because numerous federal roadblocks make cities hesitant to privatize. For example, state-owned airports can issue tax-exempt debt, which gives them a financial advantage over private airports.

In usually well-organized Germany, the new Berlin Brandenburg Airport has become a caricature of a mismanaged project. Co-financed by Berlin, the surrounding state of Brandenburg, and the federal government, the new airport was due to open in June 2012 but keeps being delayed. Construction problems crop up everywhere and costs continue to soar. Klaus Wowereit, the flamboyant previous mayor of Berlin, insisted on being chairman of the airport's supervisory board, which is one reason for many management errors along the way. In fact, Wowereit described Berlin as "poor but sexy," without realizing that Berlin's poverty had much to do with its failure to manage its assets well. In December 2014, Wowereit was forced to resign. If Berlin had had a consumer-oriented approach, the city administration would have concentrated on specifying what functionality an airport should have, and how much the city would be willing to pay every year for this functionality, and then delegated to an independent holding company or public–private partnership to invest and deliver.

Smart management can work wonders for air travelers, but also help finance airports. Singapore's Changi Airport has developed additional revenues and at the same time has emerged as a world leader in customer quality, with a five-star Skytrax rating; it is, in fact, the highest rated airport year after year. Just one example of its innovative approach is to offer a range of free services, such as guided city tours, that are supported by pay-per-use services including showers and rest zones.

Until the mid-1980s, governments owned most of the airlines, set fares and routes, and protected flag carriers by restricting new entrants. But privatization made air travel more competitive and liberalization brought competition from low-cost carriers. Most airlines in state control have failed to adapt. Many carriers are obliged to maintain lossmaking domestic routes to please politicians. Olympic Airlines was forced to deliver newspapers for a pittance to keep the country's press barons happy. The Greek national carrier went bankrupt in 2009. In contrast, Switzerland and Belgium have done fine without a flag carrier for years. Indeed, opening up to competition is likely to result in more flights and lower fares.

There are, however, a few exceptions. The thriving airlines of Singapore and Ethiopia, and the Gulf carriers, Etihad, Emirates, and Qatar Airways, all benefitted from government money but have been allowed to operate as commercial enterprises with minimal interference, although sometimes large state investments.

A related example is the Federal Aviation Administration (FAA), which is the air traffic control (ATC) service in the US. The FAA has been mismanaged for decades and provides Americans with second-rate ATC. The FAA has struggled to expand capacity and modernize its technology, and its upgrade efforts have often fallen behind schedule and gone over budget. For example, the Government Accountability Office (GAO) found one FAA technology upgrade project that had been started in 1983 and was still not concluded. Some argue that the FAA may be far too important for such government mismanagement and should be privatized. The good news is that a number of countries have privatized their ATC and could provide good models for US reforms. Canada privatized its ATC system in 1996. It set up Nav Canada, a private, nonprofit ATC corporation, which is self-supporting from charges on aviation users. The Canadian system has received high marks for efficiency, sound finances, and solid management. Better governed state-owned traffic control firms could probably aspire to similar results.

These various examples show how governments have often espoused producer rather than consumer interests when it comes to air travel. And governance of public assets has a similar bias in many other areas. A good place to start looking out for citizens and consumers is to be open about what they own.

Tell consumers what they own

Reinventing State Capitalism, a new book by Aldo Musacchio of Harvard Business School and Sergio Lazzarini of Insper, a Brazilian university, describes how the old model of Leviathan-as-entrepreneur, in which the state owned companies outright and ran them by ministerial diktat, was largely swept aside by the privatization wave of the 1980s and 90s. Yet, instead of wholesale privatization, many governments remained majority or minority shareholders and indirect investors. While this made management more professional, it also created a hazy relationship, where governments frequently failed to exercise active governance of SOEs, and also failed to stand squarely on the side of consumers or citizens.

For assets that were not converted into listed companies, the situation is mostly even less transparent. In January 2003, the GAO in the US declared that the management of federal property represented a new "high-risk" area in overall government management, due to persistent difficulties in implementing modern standards of property asset management.[1] A central land register containing all real estate assets rarely exists, or if it does, it may be, as in Germany, spread over numerous land registers kept by the local courts on the properties located in their district. Access to these registers is given only to notaries and authorities, but is not public information.

To start with, simplified reporting such as the annual reviews provided in Lithuania and Latvia can be an effective means to communicate financial overview information for government-owned portfolios. These include the aggregated portfolio value, yields, as well as breakdown data by sector, and benchmarking performance against that in similar private sector industries.[2]

In the case of the Lithuanian Annual Review, this enabled benchmarking by sector that revealed a stunning performance gap between companies owned by the government and their international competitors. Perhaps most revealing was the forestry sector, where productivity per unit of production was 30 times higher in international competitors. Even state-owned competitors were more efficient, partly because the Lithuanian state-owned forestry industry was fragmented and broken up into 42 companies, while the larger Swedish competitor, for example, was consolidated into a single company with fewer employees per hectare of forest under management. Sweden had one employee per 4,488 ha of forests under management, while Lithuania had one employee per 324 ha.[3]

Preparing and publishing such an annual review is a simple procedure requiring only a relatively short time to complete, depending on the quality of the information sources. Over time, the number and quality of information sources can also be improved. Even creating a fully professional record of the property portfolio can normally be concluded quite quickly, depending on the status of the land registry. The purpose of an intermediary, less extensive step is to create awareness of the portfolio, especially its size, composition, and overall financial performance. This can then pave the way for a more complex and comprehensive publication with the same status as a consolidated, audited annual report. Such a comprehensive annual report should include statements of the overall objectives for each entity or asset, along with financial targets and the operational targets as reported in the separate annual report of each holding. This is a simple way to ensure public capital is managed for the benefit of its shareholders (taxpayers) and within the limits of their core business.

Many countries have come some way toward better accounting practices in the government sector. A move to accrual accounting and generally accepted accounting principles (GAAP) has spread across much of the developed world and is swiftly making inroads into developing countries. Accrual accounting and GAAP standards bring greater clarity to how property-related costs and property values are recognized and measured over time. It also helps to convey a clearer understanding of why a government acquires or retains real estate and what steps are required if that need no longer exists. Accrual accounting may also assign a capital charge for holding surplus property to reflect the opportunity cost of withholding the property from its highest and best use. This forces agencies to dispose of such property in a timely manner.

Open information and proper accounting are small steps on the way toward giving priority to consumers and citizens. Separating regulatory functions from ownership is a larger and more important step.

Regulations in the interests of consumers

Economists have traditionally thought of regulation and state ownership as two alternative tools for correcting market failures. In our view this is completely mistaken. The political complications that often stand in the way of better state asset management, vested interests in the current organization, and selfish motives among those that run SOEs all imply that independent regulation of state-owned firms is needed just as much as for private firms.

The triple role of the government as a regulator, regulation enforcer, and owner of assets risks skewing the treatment granted to SOEs and serving their employees' own interests rather than consumer interests. Frequent tipping of the scales can take the form of direct subsidies, concessionary financing, state-backed guarantees, preferential regulatory treatment, or exemptions from antitrust enforcement and bankruptcy rules. In particular, regulations can easily tip over in favor of SOEs. This happens not only because a government that has taken on the responsibility for running a firm can become biased, but also because state-owned firms have an informational advantage over their political masters, and frequently use this in intense lobbying.

For these reasons, the regulation of state-owned firms is highly necessary, just as it is for private firms. For state-owned firms, however, it is even more important that the regulatory authorities should have some independence, and not be coerced by the same government ministries that act as owners of public firms. In some instances, they should probably act directly under parliament instead of under a government, just as government accountants often are.

One might argue that some laws encompass all sectors, and therefore already cover SOEs. National antitrust laws can, in principle, be used to deal with the abuse of dominant position by SOEs, even in an international context, or prevent the anticompetitive effects associated with merger and acquisition activities of SOEs.

The discipline that trade agreements and the World Trade Organization (WTO) impose on government regulations and actions does not distinguish between situations where the provider of the goods or services covered by the regulation or action is a public or a private entity. They can sometimes avert some protectionist government policies and actions involving SOEs, for example when they receive trade-distorting state subsidies. Violations of national treatment or most-favored nation principles, and the granting of subsidies or other forms of influencing trade by SOEs themselves can also be covered by WTO disciplines if these enterprises can be proven to be vested with or performing a governmental function.

Yet, overall, these general regulations hardly suffice to avoid skewed sector-specific regulations, such as banking regulations, electricity regulations, and many others. Regulations that can be abused by government ministries to favor the firms they own can have seriously negative effects on economic development. For example, in a cross-sectional study of OECD countries for the period 1975–2000, the IMF (2004) selected a number of criteria to create indices for the burden of regulation in product markets, labor regulations, taxes, and trade barriers. Improvements in these measures are significantly linked to subsequent GDP increases.

To illustrate the size of these effects, imagine a country that goes from the median of OECD countries to just barely reaching the top third in terms of growth-oriented regulations and taxes (a movement by one standard deviation in the respective index). The result, as suggested by the IMF study, would be that such an improvement in the trade barrier index would increase real GDP by 4.7% in four years; a similar change in the tax index would increase GDP by 2.3%; in the product market regulations index by 7%; and in the labor market reforms index by 1.9% during the same time span. Often these repressive regulations were instituted due to pressure from various interest groups and sometimes from SOEs that feared competition.

Part of the negative growth effect, however, may arise due to the increasing complexity of regulations. Haldane and Madouros convincingly describe this trend and its consequences.[4] In part, this complexity is driven by lobbyists' demands, and favors insiders who manage to understand the complex regulations, but also find loopholes in them. Instead, consumer-oriented regulations need to be simple and focus on outcomes and functionality instead of how things are done. SOEs should not be enticed to be lobbyists for more complex regulations on their private rivals. If regulations are applied uniformly to public and private firms alike, and by separate government authorities, then it is more likely that SOEs will also lobby for simpler and better regulations.

Governance in the name of consumers

Using the example of postal services, here we show how governments can achieve a shift toward citizen and consumer perspectives in SOEs.

In the US, the 685,000-person Postal Service faces declining mail volumes and rising costs. One alternative, advocated by some, is to privatize it and repeal the company's legal monopoly over first-class mail. Reforms in other countries show that there is no good reason for the current mail monopoly. Since 1998, New Zealand's postal market has been open to private competition, with the result that postage rates have fallen and labor productivity at New Zealand Post has risen. Similarly, Sweden has repealed the mail monopoly and turned the post office into a nonsubsidized company. Germany's Deutsche Post was partly privatized in 2000, and the company has improved productivity and expanded into new businesses. Postal services have also been privatized or opened to competition in Belgium, Britain, Denmark, Finland, and the Netherlands. Japan is moving ahead with postal service privatization, and in 2013, a 15-year liberalization process of postal services in the EU came to an end as the last member states abolished the remaining sections of the national post monopolies.

There are traditionally two major political impasses, however. First, governments would like to ensure that there is a mail service even in sparsely populated areas where mail delivery is much more expensive and not covered by the revenue generated from stamps. That has also been a traditional argument for continued government monopoly. This issue was easily solved in Sweden and elsewhere by outsourcing this specific remit and procuring the service in an open competition.

Second, there is the issue of the physical post offices themselves, often seen by politicians as one of the potent symbols of the welfare society. Countries like Sweden that exposed state-owned companies to competition early on discovered an opportunity instead. If necessary, they will pay providers for maintaining service in sparsely populated areas, without regulating exactly how this should be done. In Sweden, with huge stretches of land with few inhabitants, the fairly independent state postal company quickly figured out that the best way forward was to let grocery stores act as agents for postal services. As a result, these grocery stores are in a better position to survive. This is an example of how politicians can achieve improved outcomes for citizens by specifying and regulating what citizens need rather than trying to run a government monopoly in order to achieve social aims.

We have illustrated how governments can take quite a different tack if they start by defining what is in the best interest of citizens and consumers.

This may require some regulation, but should be nondiscriminatory, regardless of whether the providers are public or private. These public and private firms should be allowed to operate with little meddling. Publicly owned firms should be governed professionally.

In Chapter 6, we will show how governments have experimented with reforms, before we turn to our preferred method for governing public assets.

6

Early attempts to reform governance of public wealth

Many of the shortfalls in the governance of public wealth discussed in previous chapters have periodically and in some countries led to reform drives. In this chapter, we will describe how some of these have fared, starting with the most publicized and debated one, privatization. Then we move on to other types of reforms to improve management of public firms.

Waves of privatization

After the macroeconomic shocks in the 1980s and 90s, with the subsequent fall of the communist bloc, governments privatized thousands of firms,[1] opened up their economies to foreign trade, and gradually dismantled capital controls.

The first countries to undertake a long and consistent wave of denationalizations were Germany (starting in the early 1960s) and the UK (in the early 1980s). Almost all other OECD countries followed these pathfinders during the 1980s and 90s. With Margaret Thatcher as the movement's standard bearer and investment bankers from the City of London as her troops offering advice, governments in many countries reduced the size of their publicly owned sector. The privatizations mainly concerned SOEs – corporate assets owned by central government – of which several were recently corporatized former state monopolies. Concurrently, regulatory regimes were significantly reformed, from legislative, directed, detailed regulation to broader frameworks and market-oriented regulation, which also involved a marked decline in central state control.[2] Less often, privatizations involved real estate owned by the central government and, even less often, assets owned by regional and local governments.

Countries that privatized were not only aiming to promote economic efficiency in these businesses. They also wanted to support the development of capital markets, generate government revenue, and shift power from state bureaucracies to the private sector.

Even after a wave of privatization, most countries stayed in control of many SOEs and even more so their real estate assets, be it at the national or local level. In fact, in subsequent years, there was a backlash against privatization. During his presidency, Bill Clinton tried and failed to privatize the Tennessee Valley Authority. Today, such a move is not on the political agenda. But the impetus of change goes in both directions. For example, Britain considered renationalizing its railway companies a few years ago, but opted instead to deepen competition.

In some countries, privatization was precipitated by a flagrant abuse of public property. The story of Sonali Bank, Bangladesh's biggest state-owned bank, is an illustrative example. It has been robbed many times, and not only by the likes of Yusuf Munshi and his accomplices, who spent two years digging a tunnel under one of the bank's branch offices before making off with sacks of cash containing $2 million. More commonly, money goes missing in less spectacular ways. The biggest of many banking scandals in the Bangladesh banking system occurred in 2012. This particular scandal came to light when Sonali Bank revealed that one of its branches in Dhaka had illegally distributed US$460 million in loans between 2010 and 2012, corresponding to almost 1% of GDP. The largest share, or almost US$340 million, went to a single lender, of which more than 85% of those funds disappeared without a trace.

Imprudent lending, often to well-connected firms or individuals, was common among the country's banks, and Bangladesh Bank, the central bank in Bangladesh, estimated that roughly 20% of total lending from state-owned banks was in default, forcing the government to provide large injections of new capital.

Yet, there is a brighter side to this sorry tale. Officials at the central bank were doubtful that any government, despite this poor record, would be willing to privatize the four banks and part with such important sources of influence and patronage. Instead, the central bank came up with an alternative remedy, which was to increase the level of private sector competition by issuing lots of private bank licenses to restrict the growth rate of state-owned banks. As a result, the share of deposits in state-owned banks has shrunk from 60% to 25% in little more than 10 years since 1992. Instead, Bangladesh's private sector banks now hold almost two-thirds of deposits, and are the main lenders to growing private sector businesses, such as garment factories, power plants, and steel mills.

Compare that to India, which may perhaps have been spared abuses on the scale of those at Sonali Bank. As a result, there has been little public support for change. State-owned banks still control 75% of all deposits in the country. The state-owned Life Insurance Corporation of India is the largest investor in listed companies in the country, with about $50 billion invested as of September 2011.

China has tried all approaches simultaneously, including completely privatizing scores of smaller enterprises and listing large state-owned banks and enterprises, but still controls many vital SOEs. Many were seemingly modernized, submitting to the governance standards and investor scrutiny that comes with a stock market listing. But the state formally retains enough influence in more than half of these, through its controlling stakes. In practice, however, many of the formal changes to make SOEs more transparent and independent turned out to be a smoke screen, according to critics. The Organization Department of the Chinese Communist Party (CCP), effectively the HR department, remains one of the most powerful institutions in the country, with near autocratic power to appoint senior managers and plan the careers of all senior employees. This involves building varied careers for all top officials, moving them between posts in state corporations, to regional and local governments, or up to the central government level.

By law, the Organization Department appoints a party committee in each SOE and the three leading persons in each company. The chairmen of the party committee must be given a senior role, so they tend to be appointed executive chairmen in the SOEs. Even state-owned commercial banks with foreigners on their boards are said to have senior managerial appointment decisions made by the party committee rather than by the board of directors.

This close political control comes at a price, however. Many of the 155,000 enterprises still owned by central and local governments have lost ground to more agile private competitors. Faced with mounting losses in the 1990s, China implemented a first wave of reforms of its SOEs. Many were closed, others were listed on equity markets and so run a bit more like private firms. Initially, this also raised productivity and returns. But, in recent years, the state-owned sector has again been losing ground, despite the favored treatment it receives from regulators and state-owned banks.

In their recent book, *Subsidies to Chinese Industry: State Capitalism, Business Strategy, and Trade Policy*, Haley and Haley (2013) detail just how substantial state subsidies have become in many SOEs. But then, in November 2013, the CCP launched a reform plan to improve performance. As an example, Sinopec Corp. (China Petroleum & Chemical Corporation), Asia's biggest refiner, announced it would sell a US$17.5 billion stake in its retail unit to 25 Chinese groups (mainly state owned) and foreign investors, raising funds without really relinquishing the government's grip on the company. Other firms have been listed or given mandates to experiment with larger private stakes and greater independence for directors. Even local governments are announcing a flurry of similar moves.

Many countries have gone through partial or full privatizations in waves, while still trying to improve management in their SOEs by broadening the ownership or simply broadening the directors' mandate. Yet, these efforts to reform management may amount to less than they appear on paper. As Musacchio and Lazzarini (2014) describe in their book *Reinventing State Capitalism*, on paper new-style SOEs resemble true private sector firms more closely than old-fashioned nationalized industries. In practice, few have succeeded. Musacchio and Lazzarini would like to hold up Norway's Statoil as an exception and claim that it is perhaps one of the better managed SOEs in the world. In fact, in many cases, the revamped SOEs fail dismally to live up to expectations.

We now consider the case of Brazil, before we present more systematic evidence.

Brazil's attempts to reform its state behemoths

To fully understand why reforms of SOEs are so difficult in Brazil, as in many countries, it is worthwhile recollecting briefly how they came about. The many SOEs in Brazil were mainly created during two state capitalist eras. In the 1930s, an ambitious government spending program, aiming to industrialize the Brazilian economy, combined with a liquidity crunch paved the way for the creation of many large SOEs. The driving force was nationalist President Getúlio Vargas, who governed as a dictator from 1930 until 1945, and then again as the elected president from 1951 to 1954. He further expanded the sector by having SOEs charge artificially low prices, which in turn forced many owners of private sector competitors to sell their companies to the federal or state governments.

A second wave started in the 1950s to give Brazil another "big push for industrialization," when several of today's mammoth SOEs were created, including Petrobras (Petróleo Brasileiro S.A.), Eletrobras (Centrais Elétricas Brasileiras S.A.), and BNDES (Banco Nacional de Desenvolvimento Economico e Social). Petrobras was granted a monopoly for the extraction, exploration, and refining of Brazilian oil.

From the mid-1970s to the mid-1980s, under the military regime of President Ernesto Geisel and his successors, the number of SOEs grew significantly and spread to other sectors under the guise of their Second National Development Plan. President Geisel was a strong believer in state planning and sought to create SOEs in areas deemed to be "strategic assets." At this point, SOEs were established in sectors like telecommunications where existing competitors were even forced to leave the market. The exodus of private and foreign enterprises in sectors that included these "strategic assets" was reinforced by the empire building of SOE managers. An SOE in the food and grain sector could suddenly diversify its operations into the railway sector. This also hampered transparency and made these managers less dependent on federal government policies. Protected from import competition and subsidized in various ways, SOEs faced little pressure to improve their products or increase productivity. Gradually, they managed to demand ever greater subsidies, which placed a considerable burden on government finances.

Apart from national development, the SOEs also justified their subsidies on the grounds of their "social objectives," such as stabilizing prices and combating unemployment. Public sentiment in Brazil at that time was mostly positive toward these policies. It was perceived as a government's obligation to curb inflation using subsidized prices in the wake of expansionary fiscal policies.

Much of this changed in the early 1990s. Fiscal insolvency and runaway inflation was a real and present danger in the early part of the 1990s. It forced the government to reconsider its centrally planned economy, by selling public enterprises, slashing tariffs, dismantling nontariff trade barriers, deregulating foreign investment and labor markets, and removing the state from many distributive functions.

In 1992, President Itamar Franco succeeded Fernando Collor de Mello (who was impeached for corruption) and initiated a program known as the Plano Real (the Real Plan) to overhaul Brazil's economic and financial systems. The main elements of the Real Plan included introducing a new and "moderately" floating currency (the real), deindexation of the economy, an initial freeze of public sector prices, and a tightening of monetary policy. Key victories for the Plano Real program were significantly tamed inflation, where a rate of 45% in Q2 1994 was brought down to an average of less than 1% in 1996. Along with the low inflation rate, real wages increased rapidly as well. This led to booming economic activity, such as increasing domestic demand. Many SOEs were privatized during the Real Plan. President Fernando Henrique Cardoso, elected in late 1994, continued privatization into the new millennium. Indeed, between 1990 and 2002, 165 enterprises were privatized, which raised revenues equivalent to 8% of GDP, and helped repay government debt. Further steps were taken to improve the governance of SOEs, such as publicly listing them and allowing minority shareholders with at least 10% share to elect a representative on the board of directors. Figure 6.1 charts Brazil's growth from 1960 to 2011.

The various Plano Real measures were implemented from 1992 to 2002. As it played out, following the Plano Real, the period 2002–11 became Brazil's most successful ever. GDP per capita, in US$, tripled from 3,500 per year to 11,000.

In spite of this apparent success, privatization was not widely accepted. As stated before, public sentiment in Brazil supports a dominant government influence through its state-owned assets to curb inflation. During this period of privatization, left-wing political parties, SOE employers and employees, and many unions held public protests and appealed to the courts. Often the protests led to violent street rallies. Yet, the government at the time stood firm and continued with financial discipline, implementing more liberal policies, including tax cuts and floating the currency.

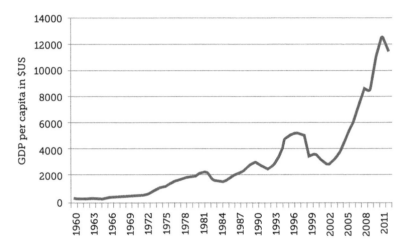

FIGURE 6.1 Rapid growth in Brazil following better governance of SOEs, privatization, and Plano Real
Source: OECD

As a measure of the success, Petrobras raised US$70 billion in the world's largest share sale during 2010, as investors bet on its plans to double output within a decade by tapping offshore fields, when many of the other global players were being challenged because their reserves were being depleted.[3] Petrobras is counting on the Tupi oil field discovery in 2006, one of the largest discoveries in Brazil and perhaps even in the western hemisphere recently. But the fall in oil prices in 2013 and 2014 is likely to upend all plans.

To some extent, orthodox Brazilian doctrine has returned under Dilma Rousseff, the current president (elected in 2010 and re-elected in 2014), who recently stated that the argument for government interference is that it is vital to "promote national champions." Far from being "promoted," however, Petrobras was forced into making large losses in the home market when it was ordered to sell fuel far below cost, which in turn required even more government subsidies and a renewed monopoly for some oil exploration. On top of this, a series of corruption and mismanagement scandals have recently been uncovered, including revelations published in a local newspaper in December 2014 by a former executive of Petrobras's refining division, who has accused more than 40 politicians of involvement in a vast kickback scheme. A series of legal actions have been filed in the US against Petrobras on behalf of investors who purchased shares in the company between 2010 and 2014. The lawsuits allege that Petrobras "issued materially false and misleading statements by misrepresenting facts and failing to disclose a culture of corruption."[4]

All in all, Brazil has converted to a free-market economy by relinquishing a large portion of its SOEs in the 1990s and improving the management in many of its remaining firms. Brazil has also been richly rewarded by experiencing a period of high growth from these and many other reforms, although in recent years, the drive for reform and growth has dissipated.

Why the new governance movement fell short

As in Brazil, many reformist governments have fully or partially privatized some SOEs. Equally important, however, have also been countries' attempts to remove the daily operation of SOEs from direct government interference. Professional boards of directors have been appointed, with fewer politicians and greater transparency. Sometimes listing on a stock market has been an instrument for forcing firms to adhere to rules of transparency and accounting standards.

This strategy has indeed improved governance. Several good examples can be found in the Netherlands. There, Schiphol, the state-owned international airport, managed to turn itself into a major hub for passenger services and an industrial center for goods that need to be delivered quickly throughout Europe. KLM, the country's flagship passenger carrier, has also been successful. The Dutch postal service became a logistics forerunner with TNT, which the German postal service tried to emulate with less success by buying DHL. Even Germany has had some success, with Lufthansa (which is profitable most of the time), while Volkswagen, which is partly owned by the state of Lower Saxony, has for generations had an active and controlling private shareholder, the Piech family that also controls Porsche, that has acted as a balance to the government shareholding with a lasting private sector influence on the company's corporate culture and development.

But many failures have also been mixed with these successes. In particular, many of the SOEs that have been given too much independence, like a child with absent parents, have engaged in highly risky international expansion (as with the German state-owned banks), making large losses. Many French SOEs are also experiencing significant losses abroad building nuclear power plants or running local transport service.

All things considered, then, this new strategy of letting SOEs operate independently as if they had no owner at all has also brought a fair share of spectacular failures. In Sweden, for example, decentralizing responsibility to the individual boards without the balancing effects of an independent professional ownership management has run into increasing troubles. The reckless international expansion by Telia, the former telephony monopoly, and Vattenfall, the former state monopoly and currently one of the largest power generators in Europe, is a case in point.

In Chapter 7, we will describe the Swedish route to reform in some detail, since it provides many insights.

chapter 7

Swedish pioneers: from active to "hands-off" governance

Sweden, an early modernizer, attempted to govern SOEs more independently from politics, although retaining significant public holdings. While, in our view, Sweden ultimately ran into a number of significant failures, it also clocked up a number of successes. Experience with the three quite different strategies that Sweden has pursued over the past few decades is instructive and is therefore told in some detail, before we move to what we see as a better approach in later chapters.

The Swedish experiment of active management, 1998–2001

In the late 1980s, Sweden was a led by a minority Social Democratic government that had studied the example of Temasek in Singapore, which we discuss in Chapter 8. In 1990, Sweden created Fortia, ostensibly a similar holding company. However, the election in fall 1991 brought a four-party, center-right coalition government to power. This new government instead put privatization policies at the top of the agenda. In three tumultuous years, during the worst of the Swedish banking crisis, it managed to privatize nearly 6% of the total state-owned portfolio. The next election in 1994 resulted in a Social Democratic minority government that primarily focused on continuing to balance state finances, but still followed through on several reforms started by the previous government.

With the newly implemented four-year parliamentary election cycle in Sweden, Göran Persson, the new Social Democratic Party leader, managed to form a minority government in spite of a smaller voter base, thanks to support from the Green and Left parties. As finance minister, Persson had resisted wholesale privatization, the prevailing international trend at the time. He continued this policy when he became prime minister in 1996, turning instead to installing active management of public assets in 1998 when the party was re-elected, for which he could gain support in the Swedish Riksdag (Parliament). He wanted to prove that governments can, indeed, be active and competent owners of commercial assets. Thus began a three-year experiment (1998–2001) of actively managing the Swedish public portfolio "as if owned by private shareholders." This included introducing private sector discipline and an equity culture, and in the end, the portfolio value increased 12% even after nearly one-third of the original portfolio was privatized, almost five times as much as when privatization was the main objective of the previous conservative government. The value increase was almost twice that of the local stock market, which rose only 6% over the same period.

A skeptical *Financial Times* reported initially on this unprecedented policy initiative for the government to act as an active shareholder of commercial assets, but gave it the benefit of the doubt, citing Sweden's strong record in managing the recent turnaround of public finances and the banking sector, after the financial collapse in the early 1990s. The editorial expressed the hope that the improved performance of public companies would open up possibilities for further privatization.[1]

The "bold, novel approach" – the first attempt by a European government to systematically address the ownership and management of SOEs – quickly yielded significant returns and benefits, as UBS Warburg described the Swedish experiment a few years on.[2] In 2000, James Sassoon and Martin Pellbäck summarized the three-year program, detailing three cases to illustrate the Swedish government's active management of public assets, including:

1 Restructuring AssiDomän, one of Europe's largest paper and packaging groups with significant holdings in forestry assets, by divesting or joint venturing portions of the industrial operations, and returning capital to shareholders.

2 Formation, restructuring, and subsequent sale of Celsius, a large European defense group, which involved finding suitable industrial partners for several of the company's business areas.

3 Transforming the state-owned rail monopoly SJ into one of the most profitable rail operators in Europe, by streamlining operations and divesting all activities other than core passenger services.

AssiDomän: from lossmaking conglomerate to focused forestry industry

Between 1992 and 1994, AssiDomän was formed from historically government-owned forestry operations in Domänverket (a state agency) and the state-owned paper and pulp producer Assi. The company was partly privatized (state ownership remained over 50%, and the remainder sold to over 590,000 individuals) through a listing on the Stockholm Stock Exchange, and become one of Europe's largest pulp, paper and packaging groups, and one of the world's largest owners of forest assets. Over the period 1994–99, the listed shares suffered from poor performance due to consecutive annual losses, lack of strategic focus, insufficient market share in several segments, and negative returns not least from massive investments and acquisitions made in the former Soviet Union. Finally, capital markets lost confidence in the company due to constant operational and financial issues, which then necessitated urgent attention from the government, its largest owner.

A new board of directors was appointed in 1999, and they hired a new CEO to implement an operational turnaround. The forestry assets were swiftly demerged, with the Swedish state swapping forest holdings for parts of its shareholding in operational units in the company. Subsequently, the industrial operations were divested or joint ventured with industrial and financial investors or partners. In 2000, the remaining pulp and paper production assets were merged with similar assets from the Swedish-Finnish forestry conglomerate StoraEnso into Billerud.

Billerud was successfully listed by year-end 2001,

which permitted AssiDomän to adjust its capital structure toward a pure forest holding company. This also resulted in a substantial one-off dividend for AssiDomän's shareholders, exceeding the entire proceeds from the Billerud IPO (initial public offering).

The Swedish government then bought the remainder of AssiDomän, as a pure forestry holding company, as part of a strategy to restructure the Swedish forestry industry, placing the delisted operations in its subsidiary Sveaskog. AssiDomän ended 2001 as one of the best performing shares on the stock market.

After all these transactions, the Swedish nation as shareholder along with the other shareholders earned an internal rate of return on its investment in AssiDomän shares over the company's publicly listed lifetime that exceeded 15%.[3] Today, Sveaskog is the largest forest landowner in Sweden, holding more than four million hectares (of which nearly three-fourths is productive), equaling 14% of the total for the country. As of 2008, the chairman of the board is Göran Persson, former prime minister.

At the outset of this experiment, many observers were skeptical of the idea of overhauling the management of public assets instead of going down the full privatization route. Halfway through the restructuring program, however, observers started to look more closely at the experiment and its potential impact on the economy. Given the portfolio's 25% share in the economy, Merrill Lynch thought the reforms would have a significant impact on Sweden's overall economic growth.[4]

Celsius: end of government reliance and the beginning of European consolidation

The demise of the Soviet Union brought shrinking defense budgets across Europe, with cooperation and consolidation high on the agenda. Celsius, the listed Swedish defense group, had a long history as a preferred supplier to the Swedish armed forces and, as such, was one of the central pillars in the country's "nonalliance" policy.

With a shrinking defense budget at home and rapid consolidation among its competitors, Celsius was seen as having limited chances for survival without considerable efficiency improvements and greater market access beyond the self-imposed statutory limitations based on Swedish non-alliance policies. The company's share price reflected this new reality, declining significantly and having a continued negative outlook. This required a radical solution by the government as the largest shareholder and key stakeholder.

The obvious route to consolidation was with Saab Group, the Swedish defense and aeronautics group, but the new board of Celsius initiated informal contacts with all relevant potential suitors that were acceptable within the restrictive Swedish foreign policy framework. To facilitate an anticipated merger, several separate divestitures were executed, since these likely would bring a higher price as stand-alone businesses, rather than being part of a larger package. These included the larger portions of Bofors (sold to United Defense Industries, then owned by Carlyle, the US private equity group, now part of BAE Systems). The shipbuilder Kockums (producing, among other things, conventional submarines with Sweden, Australia, and Singapore among its larger customers) was more difficult. The German group HDW (later merged into ThyssenKrupp), also a conventional submarine builder, seemed to be the best partner. The Germans had stronger marketing, while Kockums had developed the Stirling AIP engine, a competitive technological system enabling conventional powered submarines to operate underwater for several weeks without the need to surface, as with regular diesel-powered subs.

The divestitures eventually paved the way for the public offer by Saab Group of the remaining parts of Celsius, which is now partly owned by the Wallenberg family and BAE Systems. The Kockums' sale turned out less successfully from an industrial and national defense perspective. The submarine business was not allowed to develop properly under German ownership and was slowly withering away, with its unique technology all but ignored. This was ultimately reversed in 2014 by the Swedish government, with Saab Group taking over the original assets (including intellectual property rights) of Kockums. Originally, Saab Group had rejected the idea of adding a naval systems segment platform to its business. But now, Saab Kockum was awarded development of the next generation of Swedish submarines by the Swedish government, making Saab one of few defense conglomerates that can deliver comprehensive air, land, and sea defense solutions.

In the wider public perception, the political drama that came to surround Telia, Sweden's incumbent telecoms operator, became the poster child of a drama around the restructuring program. Merger negotiations and false starts in a proposed amalgamation with the Norwegian state-owned Telenor made for a headline-grabbing political soap opera on both sides of the border. Ultimately, the merger idea was aborted and the subsequent IPO was completed only shortly before the early 2000s dot-com bubble burst. We discuss Telia in greater detail later in the chapter.

Consolidation: creating a portfolio

The newly revamped companies faced growing global competition. Also, rapid technological development and the subsequent liberalization had exposed inefficiencies in long-held monopolies. The best of private sector discipline and a sound equity culture were needed to be able to compete on playing fields recently leveled for many new entrants worldwide. The government found itself under growing pressure from the business community and center-right opposition to privatize its extensive portfolio of commercial assets, in line with the Thatcherite winds sweeping Europe.

Prime Minister Persson, though, wanted to demonstrate to the private sector that his government could manage commercial assets as well as any private owner. As a first step in the planned three-year project, in 1998 he sought to consolidate all assets under a single command, and hired professionals from the private sector to manage ownership and the hands-on restructuring of the portfolio.[5]

Until then, the varied collection of assets had not been perceived as a coherent portfolio, nor had any of these ever been valued or governed professionally. This eclectic group of commercial companies included large former monopolies such as Vattenfall (power generation), Telia (telecoms), SJ (railway services), and Posten (postal distribution), as well as holdings in listed companies such as SAS (national airline), AssiDomän (forestry products), and Celsius (defense industry). All these operations were now to be managed under a single leadership.

However, consolidating a portfolio of commercial assets in a political environment is no easy task, as every political minister in charge of a commercial asset always seems to be keen on maintaining their fiefdom. Figure 7.1 shows the breakdown of the Swedish portfolio.

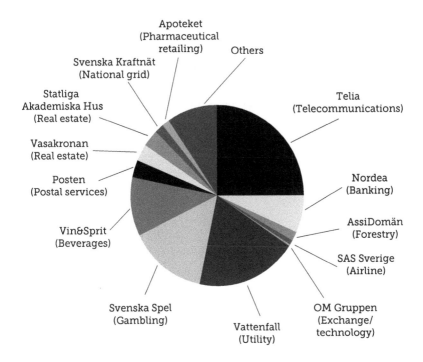

FIGURE 7.1 Breakdown of the Swedish portfolio by largest holdings

Sources: UBS; Swedish Government

At the start, shortly after the new minority Social Democratic government was formed in 1998, Erik Åsbrink, the minister of finance, refused to permit his department's holdings to be transferred to a newly designed "ownership unit" under the ministry of industry. Backing his refusal, he even threatened to leave the government, despite the prime minister's clear condition on appointing each minister that no public commercial assets were to be included in the respective departments.[6] In the end, the prime minister gave in to his finance minister (for the time being) but, nevertheless, was able to achieve nearly complete consolidation by merging several line ministries, including those for communications and employment, and industry and trade, into a single new "super ministry." This government unit was put in charge of the existing holding company Stattum, which governed most of the listed shareholdings.

The result of the first external valuation of the consolidated portfolio came as a surprise and made it possible for all stakeholders, taxpayers, financial markets, the political establishment, and the business community to understand the breadth of the portfolio and put the experiment in proper context. The consolidated portfolio could now be benchmarked against the private sector, using the overall stock market performance, against

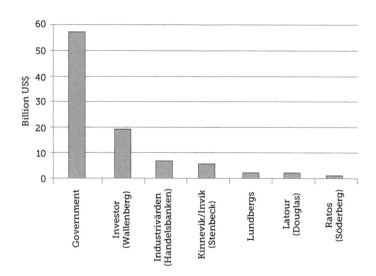

FIGURE 7.2 Largest owners in Sweden

Sources: UBS; Swedish Government

the performance of individual private sector holding companies such as Investor, Industrivärden, Kinnevik, and similar, or against any individual company within the relevant sector.

The official valuation at SEK 500 billion ($65 billion) unveiled a Leviathan seemingly overnight. State capitalism in Sweden, through union-controlled, so-called "wage earner funds," which was thought to only recently have been beaten from the ramparts, now loomed tall and dressed in a dark business suit next to the Swedish private sector. The Swedish government, or rather the nation's citizens, were now evidently, or rather "transparently," the largest owner of commercial assets in the country by far, several times larger than any individual private industrial holding group (see Figure 7.2).

Technological innovation and deregulation require restructuring

With China and India entering the global economic arena as competitors, along with rapid technological revolutions, the industrial logic of all industries changed irreversibly. A Swedish consensus arose during the late 1980s and into the 1990s, on both sides of the political divide, that the vital liberalization of infrastructure sectors was necessary to secure competitiveness in an increasingly globalized world.

Alas, some of the largest SOEs were also former monopolies. Here, the fact that the government remained owner but also regulator in the same sector (that is, the state is both player and referee) made policy rather complex. Improving the efficiency of a former monopoly also involves restructuring and reregulating the entire sector.[7]

Opening a sector to competition can be a bit like opening Pandora's box: a simple and straightforward objective uncovers a host of vested interests and hidden conflicts that politicians struggle to balance. This is one reason why many observers argue for complete privatization as the simplest way to clarify and avoid these opposing objectives, thereby enabling a swifter restructuring of the entire sector.

Issues hidden for decades inside the inner workings of a monopolistic behemoth, suddenly unveiled by liberalization, are not easy to put back into the box. This is well known in every country that has liberalized an integrated railway monopoly, postal system, or electrical power network.

Separating the railway tracks from rolling stock, and selling supporting service units to third parties has, without exception, exposed decades of mismanagement, misallocation of funds, underinvestment, corruption, and petty rivalries in every country going through this process.

Swedish State Railways (SJ): transformation from conglomerate to focused service provider

The Swedish rail services operation was originally named the Royal Railway Board until it was reformed into Statens Järnvägar (State Railways), popularly referred to simply as SJ. It was an integrated state agency responsible for operating the entire railway system in the country, receiving an annual state subsidy to cover costs for financially unprofitable operations and businesses. With no proper governance or transparency, SJ grew into an inefficient and unwieldy conglomerate, although organizationally it was still a government agency, owning diverse assets from restaurants, casinos and hotels, to ships and buses, beside its core rail-related operations.

By 1988, the Social Democratic government decided that the path to greater efficiency (and lower budgetary demands), a better service offering, and lower prices for end-users was by liberalizing the sector and opening it to competition.

The first step taken that year was separating infrastructure from operations – forming Banverket (the Swedish National Rail Administration), with responsibility for all the rail infrastructure, and retaining SJ, the old agency brand, with responsibility for operational activities.[8]

The second phase was opening both to competition, starting with local and regional traffic in 1990 and 1992, delaying until 2010 for interregional traffic. Still, Sweden was one of the first countries in Europe to largely deregulate this market.

The incorporation process was not started until the late 1990s, and revealed an unfocused organization, unused to modern service sector requirements and with an unsustainable business model. The government decided to split SJ further into three separate units: passenger services, cargo services, and a separate holding company, Swedcarrier, consolidating all noncore operations. Still, all three were directly owned by the government. This break-up was intended to allow the passenger and cargo operations to trim down into lean operators focused on their core rail services business, and prepared to compete with new entrants. The passenger operations retained the SJ brand, while the cargo service was incorporated under a new brand Green Cargo. Both operations recruited a dedicated management, preparing to meet the challenges from private sector competitors. Swedcarrier also took over the service support functions that had to transform into neutral suppliers of these functions rather than being part of the incumbent operators.

A separate board and management were appointed to Swedcarrier with experience in restructuring and divestitures. The vast real estate portfolio was concentrated in a separate subsidiary, Jernhusen, with a specialist management team charged to develop hidden values in its unique property portfolio. All noncore support services were sold to independent third parties, including IT services, train cleaning, train preparation services, maintenance, consultancy operations, and

so on. This left Jernhusen as the remaining vehicle to focus on developing the extensive property portfolio, which had previously been all but forgotten in the old agency balance sheets. Other operations sold prior to incorporation included:

- Swebus, long-distance bus services that even owned gas stations
- its shareholding in ASG, the road freight forwarding operation
- Scandlines, ferry operator between southern Sweden and the continent
- a nationwide hotel business
- a substantial restaurant business that included providing services at the largest railroad stations, in shopping malls, for on-board train restaurants, and high-end restaurants and casinos.[9]

The three-year corporate restructuring project laid bare decades of mismanagement in the sector as a whole, including underinvestment in infrastructure and rolling stock, inefficient maintenance, lack of coordination, and not least petty rivalries. Many issues remain to be resolved in the sector, including an overarching regulatory framework and institutional coordination for sector development.

It is easy to understand the inherent political resistance to restructuring public assets. Vested interests that benefit from and thrive under opacity do not voluntarily seek the light of day, nor does such a process help politicians win elections. The center-right government that came to power in Sweden in 1991 made privatization a high priority objective. And some SEK 30 billion worth of assets were, indeed, privatized during its three-year mandate.

On the other hand, although officially resisting wholesale privatization and instead embracing active ownership, the minority Social Democratic government after 1998 divested assets worth more than SEK 150 billion, in the process. This is five times as much as the earlier market-oriented government, thus taking a leaf from Thatcherism. Yet the total value of the portfolio grew significantly under the period of active ownership management, 1998–2001 (see Figure 7.3).

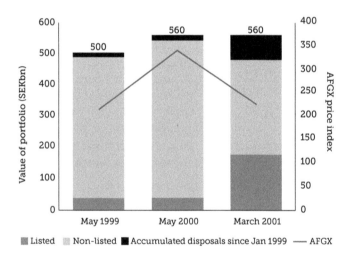

FIGURE 7.3 The Swedish portfolio beat the stock market index, including the value of divestments

Sources: Swedish Ministry of Industry; various broker estimates

Moreover, BNP Paribas[10] concluded that this metamorphosis of Swedish SOEs boosted growth in the economy over the period by improving returns from public corporations, intensifying market competition, increasing productivity and, ultimately, promoting disinflation. Indeed, as seen elsewhere in deregulating public utilities (as in telecommunications and power generation), this contributed to a significant fall in prices in these sectors from the late 1990s into the early 2000s. The "revolutionary" methods introduced in operating SOEs meant the government broke with "old-style" policies, including regulations curbing competition, ineffective capital and labor use, inventory mismanagement, and lack of transparency. Instead, SOEs were run the same as private corporations, according to BNP Paribas.

Political insulation

A unified management of a corporate portfolio in the private sector is commonly achieved by vesting all assets under an incorporated holding company. Private sector competitors owning large portfolios all have their own corporate vehicle, including the Wallenberg's (historically, Sweden's most influential industrialist family) Investor, Handelsbanken with Industrivärden, the Stenbeck family with Kinnevik and Invik (now merged), the Söderberg family's holding in Ratos, and so on. The Swedish government's reforms did not go this far. Yet, a surprise element and speed of implementation helped compensate for the lack of a proper, formal private sector-type holding company consolidating the ownership of all assets in this unprecedented active ownership approach. At least, initially.

For a start, consolidating ownership management within a single government office created a more unified and commercial ownership environment, separate from line ministries with conflicting objectives. In the absence of a strong institutional framework, active management of the portfolio was entirely dependent on the personalities in place and their informal relationships in implementing the restructuring process.

Introducing an ownership policy was vital to creating a clear chain of command from the government office, disseminating accountability and responsibilities to the appropriate levels, while attempting to inspire improvements in efficiency. Since there was no ring-fenced vehicle as primary insulation against short-term political influence, the primary legal responsibility for each company was moved to the next level – the company boards.

The governmental ownership policy helped to vest real authority in the boards with nonexecutive directors. The policy clearly limited the government's role as shareholder, to include:

- outlining the industrial vision
- setting financial objectives and performance targets
- agreeing on the appropriate capital structure and dividend policy for each holding.

Ministers also benefitted from these transparent limits to their accountability. By clearly communicating the limits of their authority over the holdings, they faced less pressure to intervene when difficult commercial decisions were taken. This worked only as long as politicians managed to keep their side of the bargain, and refrained from intervening, or even commenting, but stringently maintained the division of responsibility between political ownership responsibility and that of the board. Any suspicion or slight deviation from such an implicit contract risked ruining trust in this arrangement.

Clear objectives

The goal with restructuring was to improve portfolio performance and for the performance of each holding to be "as if owned by private shareholders." The Social Democrats in government along with their labor union allies had come to accept that globalization and technological development had completely changed conditions for the network industries such as telecoms, electricity, and many transport industries. Therefore they accepted value maximization as the sole objective of state ownership. They agreed on the motto for the three-year portfolio restructuring project – Valuable Companies Create Valuable Jobs.[11] The idea behind this motto was that an internationally competitive company was better placed to offer sustainable jobs, and perhaps also better paying jobs.

Introducing an equity culture to the management of the state-owned portfolio meant, first and foremost, that the government had to relinquish any attempt to exert short-term political influence. The company boards had to be professionalized and empowered. Maintaining credibility for this new policy was fundamental to enabling recruitment of the right professionals. Internal board evaluations were introduced to bring deeper understanding for what each holding actually needed. Despite skepticism in the business community toward actively managing state assets, many experienced, seasoned professionals stepped forward to take on nonexecutive board appointments and other types of advisory roles, in a unique spirit of collective action not dissimilar to national service.

After three years, more than 85% of the nonexecutive director positions were filled with professionals, of which more than 40% were women. Also, three in four of these companies had recruited a new CEO and half had recruited a new CFO.

Several measures were implemented to increase board effectiveness, including market-based compensation levels and a recruitment process managed by formal nomination committees based on board evaluations and the business plan requirements, and occasionally supported by outside expertise.[12] Ultimately, the management unit within the super ministry responsible for the restructuring of the portfolio built its own database and human resource capabilities for these purposes.

Transparency

Despite the lack of a formal holding company for the entire portfolio, the government managed to publish an aggregate annual report for the portfolio. This further improved transparency and helped create a sense of coherency, aligning goals between ownership objectives and the management of each holding.

In clearly separating out noncommercial operations or companies designed to address policy objectives, and only including commercial companies in the commercial portfolio, as was done in its first annual report, the minority government was able to embrace an equity culture for the commercial portfolio, and pursue shareholder value as the single objective. In this way, it was also able to garner support from across the political spectrum, even from unions.

Quarterly reporting further raised transparency standards and brought greater public scrutiny, especially from the press, financial sector and the business community, as well as from nongovernmental organizations. Annual general meetings, open to the public, further enabled external financial and industrial analysis by professionals, the media, and engaged citizens. They could now benchmark commercial SOEs against competitors in the same sector or industry.[13] Investment bankers even began to include nonlisted public assets in their equity research for comparison, and in some cases also published equity research on these as if they were listed.

Capital structure

Political acceptance of value maximization as the sole objective for the state-owned commercial portfolio was crucial. This was not driven by ideology but by a reluctant realization that all other options had been tried and failed.

Historically, government-owned companies based investment decisions on their own low cost of capital rather than the true market cost of capital. Technological developments made these inefficient, excessively capital-intensive government-owned businesses seem like lumbering dinosaurs next to the much nimbler, specialized, and focused newer entrants. Why use the post office when you can send an email? Why wait weeks for the installation of a fixed line phone when you can use a mobile phone instead? Why suffer the humiliation of delays on state railways when you can fly with a low-cost air carrier that is both cheaper and faster, or even drive in the comfort of your own car?

Being forced to deliver a return on capital created an internal cultural revolution in each holding, resulting in the hiring of the relevant professional within financial departments. Still, the otherwise dry technical tug of war between management and owners over the appropriate balance between debt and equity could sometimes spill over into the political arena. A typical bone of contention was that SOEs often tried to cling on to large reserves, excessive equity, and a bloated balance sheet as protection against hard times and a potential source of rent.

Introducing a competitive dividend policy proved an effective message to all stakeholders, emphasizing the government's intention for these holdings to operate under the same conditions as the private sector. This also applied to government plans to harmonize their capital structure with the private sector by requiring a one-off dividend.[14] Complementing this, companies were encouraged to adopt incentive schemes for their employees to align their organizations behind the owner's objective to maximize value.[15]

Broadening the stakeholder base by seeking debt funding from capital markets to a greater degree also helped instill market discipline. The financial rigor enforced by obtaining a credit rating would eventually counterbalance potentially higher borrowing costs.[16] In privatizing their debt, state-owned portfolio companies accrued many benefits of the private sector without surrendering control of any holding or its equity.

SAS: consolidating the shares of the virtual company

The share price of the three listed vehicles behind the brand name that constituted Scandinavian Airlines (SAS) has continually been traded at an unnecessary discount. The brand was owned through three separate national companies in Sweden, Denmark, and Norway. SAS was set up in 1946 as national carriers by the three governments and the Wallenberg group to establish viable regional airline services. It was then listed as three separate shares on the national stock exchanges in Stockholm, Copenhagen, and Oslo, with a complex operational agreement with all assets owned by each national company. The intraoperative agreement created a triple layer of bureaucracy (and so cost) within the company, and also tripled the number of labor union bodies management had to deal with.

The ownership structure of SAS was finally merged in June 2001, with a holding company being created in which the holdings of the governments changed to Sweden (21.4%), Norway (14.3%), and Denmark (14.3%), and the remaining 50% publicly held and traded on the stock market. The ownership restructuring not only involved complex operational and financial issues, but also significant diplomatic challenges including landing and fly-over rights. These had to be renegotiated in unprecedented multilateral negotiations. After months of wrangling, preparations, negotiations, and coordination between the various stakeholders at different levels within a highly complex process, the airline was merged into a single company with a single share, reducing decades of complexity into something a bit more transparent.

The three-party merger had the desired positive impact on the share price and paved the way for significant improvement in operational efficiency. It was also a vital step that enabled participation in the wider industry consolidation. But in the end, the Norwegian government at that time resisted these invitations of a wider European consolidation, blocking any potential transaction, since the government stakes remain bound by a shareholder agreement.

As a national carrier, it is still far from the lean cost structure and organization of its low-cost competitors, such as Norwegian Air, the regional champion, which have changed the industry landscape. Overcapacity in the industry and its unfavorable cost structure has imposed losses on SAS, forcing it to return to capital markets for regular capital injections, and always promising yet more cost cutting and structural reform.

The three government owners currently agree to participation in European airline consolidation, but this is now a much more difficult proposition.

Streamlining and developing a core business in each holding

Companies with a dominant market position can generate significant profits. In the absence of an active, professional shareholder with strict requirements for return on capital and dividends, management instinctively hides these profits through complex accounting, or excessive costs or investment. The logical consequence is empire building by integrating the business vertically or horizontally – instead of surrendering dividends.

In SOEs, this instinct is reinforced by the practical complication of raising additional capital when required. Compared to privately owned businesses, SOEs that need additional funds are subject to a cumbersome, time-consuming political process, often involving formal parliamentary attention. In this process, the commercial merits of the request for capital are weighed against other uses for tax revenue. So investment is compared to policies ranging from childcare and schools to highways and national defense. Also, by necessity, requesting funds from government and parliament must follow the political calendar, a process insensitive to market requirements or the simple time value of money.

Mostly, the Swedish reform of SOE governance helped insulate them from short-term political influence and introduced an equity culture with a focus solely on maximizing value. This allowed managers to concentrate operations on high value-added activities, and drop unprofitable ones. Activities unrelated to a core business would only distract management attention from its purpose, necessitating divestment. Like any talented athlete, managers now understood they could not be both a leading marathoner and, say, a boxer at the same time. Senior management couldn't claim to be expert at a range of aspects and opportunities in businesses completely unrelated to their core skills, so they ultimately had to choose.

Posten: the metamorphosis of a utility

Sweden was the European nation that took deregulation of postal services the furthest when it fully liberalized its postal market as early as 1993. Deregulating this market was similar to that of the telecommunications market, with dramatic changes to the market due to rapid technological developments across national borders and in terms of pricing, services offered, efficiency, and market players.

The mail division of Swedish Posten AB was one of the most efficient postal operators in Europe at that time, second only to TPG, the Dutch national post office. But its opportunities to export this competitive advantage to other European countries were limited.

In addition, letter-related operations were under threat from increased competition and substitution by new forms of communication, namely the Internet. Posten's low profitability and high operating leverage, coupled with the fact that it was operating in a liberalized market, made it vulnerable to "cherry picking" by new entrants, especially as the new entrants were not required to offer a universal service.[17]

Just before Christmas in 1998, the management of Posten demanded a substantial capital injection from the owner, or else, it claimed, the company would go bankrupt. The owners reacted swiftly to the threats with a financial review and audit of the company over the Christmas holidays. This clearly showed that the company's balance sheets did not need additional capital, but rather it needed a simplified accounting structure, financial restructuring, and stronger focus on its core business.

A new board was appointed and found a course through the challenging uncharted waters. After a minor skirmish with its owner regarding the scope of its core business and the definition of "logistics," it was able to concentrate fully on consolidating its balance sheets and focus operations by divesting all noncore assets. This started with the payment clearing system, PostGirot, which was restructured to adapt to the banking system and sold to the market listed bank, Nordea (also partly state owned), and was followed by the sale of a controlling stake in ASG, a larger listed road transport and logistics provider in Sweden, to Deutsche Post logistics subsidiary Danzas (which later merged with DHL and took that internationally known brand as its name). Posten also sold a number of several lesser holdings to different buyers and a real estate portfolio to Deutsche Bank Private Equity.

Most importantly, Posten managed an epic strategic transformation in a very short time frame and with limited political friction. It has gone from owning a wide network of common "post offices" to now outsourcing almost all its retail operations through a franchise network of so-called "service points" in supermarkets, grocery shops, and petrol stations. The political effort to support this transformation was no less impressive, as the local post office was seen as a historically vital symbol in tying sparsely populated rural areas in such a geographically large nation to each other, and to the center, and was considered a key pillar in building Sweden's modern welfare society. Proactively dismantling such a potent symbol, with its many strongly unionized public employees, took considerable political will, consensus, and an insightful union and political leadership. The unions were supported by the so-called "Telia model," a skills renewal scheme offering employees the opportunity, during their notice period (and possibly longer), to focus full time on finding a new job, with access to professional support, on-the-job training, office premises, and related tools.

> An early ambition to consolidate postal operations finally came to fruition in 2009 when Posten merged with Post Danmark to form PostNord, with the Swedish government holding a 60% share and the Danish government holding the remaining 40%.

Following the concept of "good bank/bad bank" learned in handling the early 1990s banking crisis, noncore assets were often separated into a discrete holding company for restructuring, having different managers and business objectives, specializing in restructurings and divestitures. Such a separation allowed the management of the core business to concentrate fully on developing this without any concern for the restructuring of the noncore parts. The noncore holding companies were either directly owned by the state, as with the railway monopoly SJ, or they were kept inside the group but with additional private equity-type shareholders brought in to provide specialist skills, such as for the telephone operator Telia.

More than a third of the entire portfolio of commercial assets was divested during the three-year restructuring program, including the IPO in Telia and a remaining shareholding in the NYSE-listed pharmaceuticals group Pharmacia & Upjohn, which was sold at an all-time high. Several of the listed shareholdings, where the government had a majority stake, underwent significant restructuring during the program, including SAS, Celsius, and AssiDomän.

From active to "hands-off" governance

While the active restructuring was surprisingly successful, it may also have seemed like a streak of luck to many Swedish politicians. Success relied heavily on a clear mandate and intention from the prime minister, and a competent team. Neither could be relied on to prevail forever. Perhaps for these reasons the Swedish government gradually changed tack, and moved from active ownership to a "hands-off" approach. Developments in Telia illustrate this change and its consequences.

Telia: the mobile phone pioneer with interrupted international ambitions

During 1998, Lars Berg, CEO of Telia (the successor to the government-owned Televerket telephony monopoly), had taken it upon himself to agree to sell the government's shareholding, without prior approval of the owner, or knowledge of his senior managers, or the board of directors. He conducted negotiations singlehandedly in order to maintain secrecy, with no owner mandate and none of the standard processes normally involved in commercial transactions of this nature – including due diligence and external valuation or strategic review confirming the operational, commercial, and financial validity of the transaction. The chief executive had simply come to agreement with the Norwegian government on merging Telia with the Norwegian state-owned telecoms incumbent, Telenor, and set an arbitrary price on the shares without any external or internal valuation. The agreement was uncovered in the early days of the new active management of the government portfolio and surprised everyone on the Swedish side from the chairman and CFO to the prime minister.

To avoid an embarrassing situation for both governments, professional discussions between them were initiated under the greatest secrecy. The Swedish government hired the relevant professional advisers and introduced a fully fledged professional process to assess the commercial viability of the potential transaction and attain a correct valuation of the two parts to be merged. Lars Berg left the company and was replaced by an executive from Ericsson, the Swedish communications technology and services provider. When the merger process did not follow Norwegian intentions, including their efforts to discuss financially based rather than ad hoc valuations, the confidential discussions broke down. Insiders started to leak the content of the discussions to the press in a likely attempt to force the Swedish government's hand.

Once the commercial discussions were out in the open, what followed turned into a politically driven process that involved almost a year of mud-slinging in the media between the two governments. But it wasn't until the very end that the secret Norwegian ambition to capture the Swedish mobile phone research department (this was during the tech stock boom), seen then as one of the strongest in the world, was revealed. It became apparent that the basic driving force for the merger on the

Norwegian side was the potential relocation of this pioneering research group as the cornerstone establishment in a Norwegian technology park that was being built outside Oslo.

In the end, the merger fell apart in December 1999, and Telia then pursued a merger with Sonera, the recently listed incumbent Finnish mobile telephony company, also partly owned by the government. As Sonera was already listed, Telia also needed to be in order to get a fair market value prior to any merger and especially to avoid possible public criticism of the exchange value assigned to the company.

Sonera shares had skyrocketed in the early hours and days after its IPO, the year before. The company became a favorite among investors looking for investments in the popular telecoms sector. However, the massive transfer of wealth from the government and its taxpayers to the new shareholders was heavily criticized, causing a government crisis and the dismissal of the responsible minister and the company chief executive.

The Swedish government, nervous about repeating this Finnish mistake, consequently ordered an aggressive pricing for the Telia IPO so as to avoid similar accusations of selling state assets too cheaply. Moreover, the political instincts of the Social Democratic minority government to combine an aggressive pricing of the IPO with marketing the privatization of this SOE as a "people's share," where the general public were actively encouraged to participate in the share offering (with a first option to buy and similar), resulting in an unprecedented 10% of the population buying into the company, led to unintended political consequences.

From a financial perspective, the Telia IPO was an unqualified success for the government and, for that matter, taxpayers too. Completed in June 2000 at the tail end of the tech stock bubble, share trading remained stable even through the turbulence caused by the subsequent stock market crash, largely due to the positive market outlook for the company.[18] After a professional process and commercial discussions, the boards of the two listed incumbents, Telia AB and Sonera Oy announced their planned merger in March 2002. The new company, TeliaSonera, was then 37% owned by the Swedish government and 13.2% by the Finnish government, with the rest mostly owned by institutional investors in addition to the many Swedish retail owners.

From a political perspective, market ups and downs do not win votes. The bursting of the tech stock bubble also hit the Telia stock price hard, demonstrating the disadvantage of selling shares in a listed company to the general public, as if the shares were a risk-free sovereign bond. This stigma stuck to the Social Democratic government throughout the rest of its term, with almost 10% of the electorate feeling the financial consequences of the government's actions as an owner of commercial assets written on the price of the stocks.

From a commercial perspective, the merged company initially continued on its path of focusing on its core business and improving operational efficiency after the three-year active ownership project. However, in the absence of a permanent institutional framework to replace the active ownership project and a lack of stricter demands on its capital structure, it eventually ended up acquiring assets in remote places far from its core competences and markets, without any insight into these operations or assets. This brought financial, legal, and political repercussions that are still impacting its business.

This is exemplified by the episode leading to the resignation on February 1, 2013 of TeliaSonera's then CEO, Lars Nyberg. This came after the law firm the board had hired to investigate accusations of graft reported that the company should have been much more careful in purchasing a phone license in Uzbekistan in 2007. The investigation was called for after Swiss prosecutors froze $900 million linked to Gulnara Karimova (the daughter of Uzbekistan's President Islam Karimov) and a mobile operator. TeliaSonera has also disclosed that Dutch authorities asked it to post collateral of between €10 and 20 million for potential financial claims against its local holding company. The investigation has widened to included prosecutors in Switzerland and the US as well as Sweden, who are also looking into allegations that TeliaSonera paid SEK 2.3 billion ($358 million) for a 3G license in Uzbekistan in 2007 to Takilant, a Gibraltar registered firm, when it knew the company was a front for Karimova and her family.

The allegations, first made in a Swedish television program in 2012, have not only forced Nyberg to leave, but also most of the company board and several senior managers. TeliaSonera could also have heavy fines imposed if found guilty of violating US laws and Securities and Exchange Commission regulations.

In addition, a separate review by the new TeliaSonera board into its other transactions in its Eurasian unit (including Moldova, Georgia, Azerbaijan, Kazakhstan, Tajikistan, and Nepal) has found that the form of these deals was similar to that in the Uzbekistan transactions, so further revelations from the company are expected. Johan Dennelind, the new chief executive (since September 2013) who was hired to clean up the telecoms operator, has since appointed a new chief compliance officer and general counsel, and introduced an anti-corruption program within the firm.

The missing link: the holding company and what happened after 2001

A company with the government as shareholder will always be perceived as "state owned" regardless of the shareholding size. We've noted that politicians can never be ideal shareholders, as their concerns are so much broader than value maximization. Meddling in the affairs of SOEs will likely be ill-informed at best, opportunistic at worst. But passive or hands-off ownership is not good either. As the example of Telia illustrates, this leaves a governance vacuum. This vacuum is often filled by management that then assumes the role of both owner and manager.

In this context, a ring-fenced holding company assigned a simple, single, clear objective has the benefit of enabling the holding company to represent taxpayers and its agents (the government) with a clear and distinct voice – as a professional corporate governor.

The intractable conflict of interest between the government role as regulator and its role as owner of a going business in a deregulated, liberalized industry sector would also be resolved using this kind of separate, ring-fenced ownership vehicle, according to an official Swedish government report on liberalization and regulation. The report emphasized that such a holding company should also have an owner in the government separate from any line ministry involved with regulation.[19]

A similar conclusion was reached by a Swedish government report on ownership governance of central government assets. The report concluded that an independently accountable professional organization for corporate operational administration should be established as a link between the political and strategic governance from parliament and the government on the one side, and the individual portfolio companies on the other, aiming to generate value and handle operational governance.[20]

Sadly, Swedish governments failed to act on these insights. Governance of state-owned firms deteriorated during the new millennium. A hands-off approach without the institutional framework allowing for a more permanent active governance let loose ill-advised excesses. Vattenfall is the most egregious example in Sweden.

Vattenfall: from local to European giant

In October 2014, Vattenfall, one of the largest energy producers in Europe, announced an increase in the previously envisaged write-down, now amounting to SEK 53 billion (US$6.8 billion), which is more than 10% of total assets. This is primarily related to the 2009 acquisition of the Dutch company Nuon.[21] Vattenfall's value has halved in recent years, according to estimates by Swedbank, from at most SEK 400 billion (US$51 billion) to about SEK 200 billion currently.[22]

These huge losses have had political repercussions, not least due to the size of the total value erosion, exceeding 1% of Sweden's GDP. Even before the latest write-downs, the company felt forced to split into two divisions: one for the Nordics and one for Europe. This was seen as an attempt to soften criticism ahead of elections held in September 2014, and allowing the (ultimately) responsible prime minister to note this would enable selling a minority stake in the company.[23]

Vattenfall, like many European power generators, has been weakened by huge debts accumulated during a decade of takeovers sparked by the liberalization of European energy markets in the 1990s, and was poorly prepared for the eurozone crisis and upheaval in the energy market. It announced 2,500 job cuts in 2013, mainly in Germany and the Netherlands, with further job losses expected and investment cutbacks over the next five years to save margins.

Deregulation in Sweden started in 1996 and a final phase was introduced in 1999. Introducing private sector discipline and an equity culture that came with the restructuring the government portfolio, starting in 1998, was an alien concept to the dominant player in the Swedish power market. The newly appointed Vattenfall board at that time was quick to instill a more commercial perspective on both the capital structure and the cost of capital, thereby sharpening its strategic focus. The board also quickly decided to divest noncore assets that could not provide acceptable returns, not the least in remote geographical locations ranging from South America to Southeast Asia. The new focus involved staying strictly commercial, with a geographic concentration in countries around the Baltic Sea.

The introduction of a new regulatory regime in Germany and the EU gave rise to several opportunities to acquire major assets in northern Germany, such as shares in publicly held companies in Berlin and Hamburg, and in assets in Poland and Finland. Within two years, Vattenfall had become the third largest power generator company in Germany. However, several of these acquisitions involved acquiring brown coal-fired power plants, and brown coal mines, which are now controversial sources of energy due to high CO_2 and other pollutant emissions.

The 2009 agreement to buy Nuon, the Dutch utility company, was an acquisition worth almost SEK 97 billion (nearly $14 billion at the time). Following this acquisition, Vattenfall started to divest parts of businesses in Denmark and Poland to focus on three core markets: Sweden, the Netherlands, and Germany.[24]

Then, in 2013 and 2014, Vattenfall announced the historic write-downs, raising a major political debate in Sweden concerning government ownership, and the management and viability of the board. Questions were raised about the inside details behind the largest transaction ever undertaken by an SOE in Sweden, including how the chief executive of Nuon became chief executive of Vattenfall and the nature of his compensation related to the transaction.

If the government approved the acquisition, as prescribed by the ownership policy, this also raises the question of whether it was an appropriate use of public funds and if government ministers are best placed to determine such financial issues. We therefore ask whether the value destruction this deal has entailed could have been avoided if these government assets had been governed through an independent holding company that was properly incentivized to enforce a stricter active ownership, a commercial capital structure, and a competitive dividend policy. Further, was something amiss in the regulatory framework so that monopoly profits were used for expansion rather than reinvestment?

In Chapter 8, we turn to Singapore, a country that made an early attempt with an active holding company for public assets.

chapter 8

"Hands-on" but independent governance: the innovator from Singapore

Before we describe Singapore's experience in detail, consider first a number of factors that have contributed to interest in a hands-on, but more independent governance of public wealth.

During Sweden's early success with enlightened active management of public assets, international observers were watching with great interest. In 2000, Lord Sassoon, then an investment banker at UBS Warburg, predicted that the Swedish experiment was likely to be followed by many others as pressures for efficiency, prudence, and transparency in the government sector increased. The Swedish approach was used as a model for the UK government's Shareholder Executive, which was established in September 2003 as part of the Cabinet Office. Today, it is part of the Department for Business, Innovation and Skills. Subsequently, Norway and Finland revised their state ownership policy. Norway set up a similar unit as the earlier Swedish government, while Finland established Solidium in 2008, a holding company for its listed companies.[1, 2] Further away, China was to emulate this approach by setting up the State-owned Assets Supervision and Administration Commission of the State Council, a special ministry for its SOEs, and Central Huijin Investment Ltd as the holding company for its state-owned banks.

The initiative was also presented at an OECD meeting in Budapest in 1999 and strongly supported and lauded by the British representative as "something worth emulating by other member countries," while the southern European representatives all but dismissed the initiative, claiming that they "would be shot if tried in my country." Nevertheless, the OECD managed to unite all member countries in an agreement to emulate the lessons from the Swedish experience, including the idea of consolidating all assets under a single ownership management, and in 2005 established the OECD Guidelines on Corporate Governance of State-owned Enterprises, with the IMF and the World Bank as observers.[3]

These kinds of reactions to hands-off, active governance mirrored a major metamorphosis of how private corporations were governed. A more recent sea change has moved toward a more active, professional governance of private firms.

How the private sector reformed governance

The managerial revolution in the early 20th century went in the opposite direction, however. This was driven by a large-scale shift in ownership from private individuals to large anonymous institutions such as pension funds and insurance companies. Since these were mostly passive, real power over many large corporations moved from the owners to managers. Corporations became conglomerates, even empires, with a growing share of the return on assets being eaten up by inefficiency and swelling organizational coffers rather than accruing to shareholders. Managers were rarely challenged and enjoyed long periods of employment. And they were allowed to amass corporate wealth in the form of cash reserves and subsidiaries that could be sold if necessary. This often led to low profitability and low productivity growth.

During the late 1980s and into the 1990s, large shareholders increasingly reasserted control.[4] Corporate raider, private equity, and activist shareholders benefitted from the bloated balance sheets and complacent institutional investors. The cross-holding of shares was virtually abolished in many countries. Managers were still being paid substantial amounts, but with compensation often coupled with results, the pressure to perform had risen and the turnover of managers increased.

Importantly for our argument, owners also systematically forced managers to relinquish corporate wealth. Conglomerates were often broken up and noncore subsidiaries sold. Cash reserves were paid out to owners as higher dividends. Owners forced corporations to "sweat" their assets, in effect returning more of the corporation's reserves to shareholders, at the risk of hostile takeovers. Corporate real estate portfolios were consolidated and managed under a single management and coherent strategy and often ultimately divested. Corporations were forced into leaner balance sheets with higher leverage. With less wealth at their disposal, managers could not easily hide poor performance by drawing on reserves. The opportunities and incentives to misuse corporate wealth for personal gain or wield influence in relation to shareholders were greatly reduced.

This dramatic change in corporate governance went hand in hand with an improvement in productivity growth and profitability in much of the western world. So, we think it useful to examine whether the same type of change would work with public assets. Politicians with less easy access to public wealth might do a better job of governing their country for the common good. In fact, we see that this has already taken place in some areas.

Good examples from the public sector

In some respects, removing wealth from direct political access has not only been adopted in many countries, it has also become rather uncontroversial. A prime instance of removing national assets from political control involves central bank independence from direct political control. Many countries have adopted this stance during recent decades. International organizations, including the World Bank, the Bank for International Settlements, and the IMF, strongly support central bank independence.

In cases where governments have used central banks as cash machines, as in Zimbabwe after 2000, they quickly create hyperinflation. The more common and subtle problem, though, is that a central bank may maintain excessively low interest rates, thus encouraging wage inflation or a credit bubble, when they are too susceptible to political direction or pressure. Governments generally have some degree of influence over ostensibly "independent" central banks. For example, the board of governors of the US Federal Reserve are nominated by the US president and confirmed by the Senate, clearly a political process.

Several studies[5] have found that independent central banks are better at controlling inflation. Not all economists agree, particularly as to whether these findings merely show correlation or an actual causal connection. But very few would argue that independence is a disadvantage.

Funded public pension systems have also benefitted by removing management from direct political influence. Frequently, public pension funds have been mismanaged and performance, as measured by most reasonable standards, has been poor. Around the world, reserves in partially funded public schemes have been used to subsidize housing, state enterprises, and various types of economically targeted investments.[6] They have been used to prop up stock markets and as a captive source of credit, and they have probably allowed governments to run larger deficits than would otherwise be possible. Investment decisions are typically made in a regulatory vacuum, with little public accountability, limited access to information, and obscure management processes. To find examples, one can to go back to Hitler's large drain of public pension funds to finance arms and highways. Unfortunately, there are many more recent examples, such as Argentina, where the government has raided public pension funds.

In attempting to improve the management of public pension funds, many countries have moved toward isolating them from direct political control and demanding more transparency and accountability. In Canada, the finance minister now appoints the 12 members to the Canadian Pension Plan Investment Board, in consultation with provincial governments. The appointment process involves a nominating committee that recommends qualified candidates for the federal and provincial governments to consider. The board and the appointment process are subject to close public scrutiny, and candidates for the board, in addition to having suitable qualifications, must meet skill and character requirements.

New Zealand has chosen full disclosure of governing routines. Under New Zealand law, the minister has explicit power to direct the governing board of the public pension fund. However, directions must be submitted in writing, presented to Parliament, and published in the official gazette.

How can these examples be applied to the governance of SOEs? In fact, a few countries have successfully adopted a similar approach. Austria gathered many SOEs under the umbrella of ÖIAG, an independent holding company, with bylaws that explicitly forbid politicians from sitting in the board of directors. However, one of the earliest attempts was made in Asia.

Temasek: the pioneer from Singapore

On 6 February, 2009, it was announced that Charles "Chip" Goodyear, former CEO of BHP Billiton, the largest global mining company, was to become the first foreign CEO of Temasek Holdings. He was made a board member in February and CEO-designate in March, and then in July it was confirmed that he would not be CEO. The (soon-to-be aborted) appointment was immediately welcomed as a move to inject fresh blood into Temasek, the largest and most prominent Asian investment company. Goodyear had years of experience in the commodity sector, causing speculation that his appointment was intended to help Temasek enter the natural resource and energy sectors just as rising demand from China presented opportunities. This appointment was extraordinary because Temasek is the wholly owned government holding company for Singapore, and Goodyear was neither from Singapore nor a politician, he was simply a well-known US business executive hailing from Louisiana.

Temasek was incorporated in 1974 in Singapore to manage government ownership in strategic industries that had previously been held directly under the Ministry of Finance. Following independence in 1965, as part of its industrialization plans to jump-start the nation's economy, the government had taken a proactive role in establishing SOEs in key sectors like manufacturing, finance, trading, transportation, shipbuilding, and services. Early companies were Keppel, Sembawang, and Jurong Shipyards (spurring Singapore's development into a major shipbuilding and refitting center). Neptune Orient Lines was established as a shipping company to leverage the island's strategic location in one of the world's busiest passages between Europe/Middle East and North Africa and East Asia.

The aim of outsourcing the governance of these commercial assets was to free government to focus on overarching economic issues, while encouraging a commercially disciplined and independent holding company to achieve sustainable long-term returns. In 1972, Goh Keng Swee, then deputy prime minister and credited as the founder of Temasek and often called the "economic architect" of Singapore, said in an essay on economic development:

> One of the tragic illusions that many countries of the Third World entertain is the notion that politicians and civil servants can successfully perform entrepreneurial functions. It is curious that, in the face of overwhelming evidence to the contrary, the belief persists.[7]

Two more holding companies, MND Holdings and Sheng-Li Holdings (now Singapore Technologies), were set up post-independence. The latter is responsible for defense-related holdings, but both were subsequently consolidated into Temasek.

Today, Temasek sees itself as an Asian investment house headquartered in Singapore. In response to the international perception of Temasek as a sovereign wealth fund (SWF), its CEO-designate Chip Goodyear commented in 2009:

> Don't muddle Temasek with sovereign wealth funds. Those guys work on cash reserves. The local example would be GIC [the Government of Singapore Investment Corporation], which was set up to invest the nation's spare cash. As an investment firm we don't like to keep spare cash ... We were set up to manage a portfolio, invest shareholder funds, and raise funds to grow the portfolio.[8]

Temasek was set up as a holding company designed to separate the regulatory and policy-making functions of government from its role as a shareholder of commercial entities.[9] It has succeeded in consolidating all the commercial assets owned by the government, apart from large holdings in property. This makes it a uniquely focused national wealth fund (NWF) compared to other Asian countries, which have a propensity to create multiple NWFs, as has been done in Malaysia and Abu Dhabi.

Critics have sometimes claimed that behind the stated commercial objective is a camouflaged political objective. The government might be using Temasek and its portfolio of SOEs, or as they prefer in Singapore, GLCs (government-linked companies), including its shipping firms, the DBS Bank, Singapore Technologies Engineering, and Singapore Telecommunications (Singtel), as an engine for national economic growth.[10] The value of Temasek represents more than half of national GDP, indicating the dominant position of power it has in Singapore. Correspondence leaked from the US Embassy in Singapore discussed this influence as being so dominant that it involves a reverse dependency – where the government of Singapore takes instructions from Temasek.[11] The value of Temasek and the Government of Singapore Investment Corporation (GIC) together exceeds the entire economy measured as GDP, making them, by definition, extremely important to the success of the country.

Temasek's growth attracts criticism both domestically and from abroad. Through the company, the Singapore government dominates the local stock market, controlling nearly 20 of the largest listed companies. And working for Temasek is often jokingly referred to as "doing your national service." While the SOEs were originally established to act as catalysts for national industrialization, they have since expanded into all areas of the economy, including those served by private business. Domestically, many, including some in government, question this dominance and the risks it entails of crowding out private sector initiatives. In this sense, Singapore took a different approach from the other Asian tigers (Taiwan, South Korea, and Hong Kong), where economic success was built on private entrepreneurship rather than state-owned capitalism. The Singapore government is now actively attempting to balance this problem by stimulating entrepreneurship.

Internationally, the Singapore government is perhaps more keen to prove that Temasek and its SOEs are run commercially rather than on ideological grounds, that is, with no state interference or favors. The companies are expected to be efficient and profitable and receive no special privileges or concealed subsidies. Yet time and again, charges surface that the SOEs receive favoritism at the expense of private enterprises. An IMF study investigated the potential benefits of being a GLC to explain the premium often paid on GLC share prices, but did not find any evidence of favorable treatment apart from the brand recognition of being a GLC.[12] Nevertheless, when considering further international expansion, the issue of political independence remains a significant sore spot for Temasek.

In the early 1980s, Temasek and the GLCs were consciously molded into profitable and internationally competitive organizations, so that each holding was capable of investing and expanding internationally. The portfolio increased in value from S$345 million in 1974 to S$2.9 billion in 1983, covering 58 firms with over 490 subsidiaries. International growth in key holdings provided Temasek with growing knowledge of regional markets along with its holdings. This paved the way for broader international expansion of its portfolio many years later.

In Temasek's second phase, from the mid-1990s, the Singapore government liberalized a dozen sectors. Temasek grew by taking over newly incorporated key services, national utilities, and infrastructure assets, including telecommunications, ports, and power supply, and listing them on the Singapore Stock Exchange.

Temasek's third strategic phase started in 2002 with the appointment of Ho Ching, then hailed as the first professional CEO of Temasek. Previously, only senior civil servants had held this position. But the appointment was widely criticized, because Ho Ching was married to Lee Hsien Loong, son of Singapore's founding Prime Minister Lee Kuan Yew, who then become prime minster himself in 2004. Many also argued for her appointment, stating that it was necessary in order to bring about a significant commercial reorientation and internationalization of the company, with a stronger focus on shareholder value and a divestiture of noncore assets. Ho Ching spearheaded aggressive expansion abroad in several sectors, including financial services, property, and technology, media and telecommunications (TMT). One obvious reason for foreign diversification was that the former monopolies had been opened to competition and foreign ownership, which was expected to lower Temasek's yield.[13] It is also possible that further domestic growth conflicted with government policies to foster private sector entrepreneurship.

Prior to the very brief appointment of Chip Goodyear in 2009, the company had experienced some setbacks. Most visible were its significant investment in many of the biggest global banking names. Some of these stakes were neither related to its core interests in the sector, nor deemed particularly operational in nature or large enough to allow for active management. During the financial crisis of 2008–09, Temasek lost nearly one-third of its portfolio value – a huge blow to its credibility as an active, professional investor, although it pretty much followed global stock market trends.

The other setback was a political backlash around several international investments. Despite its respected governance, transparency, and professional management, Temasek was still seen by many as a vehicle to pursue the national interests of its sovereign shareholder.[14] An attempt to buy a stake in Shin Corporation, owner of significant broadcasting rights in Thailand, from former Prime Minister Thaksin Shinawatra caused popular resentment in Thailand. Antitrust authorities in Indonesia charged Temasek with monopolizing the telecommunications market, even though it only had indirect minority holdings and used a local partner (the Indonesian government). Also, an investment in Optus, a technology services firm with Australian defense contracts, fuelled international concern that Temasek was a political vehicle for the Singapore government.

Temasek's intentions in the US were also questioned, although it has been a significant investor in the country for years, pouring funds into several banks (such as a $4.4 billion investment in Merrill Lynch), Silicon Valley startups, and various private equity and hedge funds. Several of Temasek's portfolio companies also have significant US operations, for example Singapore Technologies Telemedia, a wholly owned subsidiary, which owns two-thirds of Global Crossing (and employs more than 2,000 people in the US), and California-based American President Lines (APL), the world's seventh largest container transportation and shipping company and wholly owned by Neptune Orient Lines (where Temasek holds a two-thirds interest). APL operates ports in three western states and is the Department of Defense's second largest cargo carrier, employing more than 3,100 people in the US. Another is VT Systems, a wholly owned subsidiary of Singapore Technologies Engineering, with more than 4,000 US employees, and a leading supplier of sophisticated technology and mission-critical goods to the US armed forces.[15]

Here, the main issue is political independence. Temasek is formally held through the Ministry of Finance, while the CEO, Ho Ching, is the wife of Prime Minister Lee Hsien Loong. Her appointment was originally criticized for not being based on merit, but for corrupt nepotistic motives – the advancement of the Lee family interests. Recruiting

Goodyear was meant to remedy this perception and provide much sought-after political independence in order to improve the company's institutional credibility. But Goodyear resigned after only six months on the board. The reasons for his departure are not publicly known, other than the official statement that there were "differences regarding certain strategic issues." Reportedly, his suggested changes to the management board and initiatives for a new strategic direction were poorly received, some even arguing that his proposals for a new strategy were too risky.[16]

The latter fed into theories circulating at Goodyear's departure that he was unable to persuade the board in regard to investing in his area of expertise – mining and natural resources. A move into mining might have been seen to jeopardize Singapore's closer relationship with China, putting the country in direct competition with China for assets in the natural resource sector – one that is crucial to fuelling Chinese economic expansion.[17]

Sources close to the Singapore government said there had been "a clash of cultures" with Suppiah Dhanabalan, Temasek's chairman, who, in July 2009, was quoted as saying:

> A future CEO has to be someone who understands and shares our values, and who is also a builder of people, institutions and opportunities. Unfortunately, at this halfway mark, both the board and Chip have come to the conclusion that it is in our mutual interest not to proceed with the planned leadership change.[18]

Temasek was established as an operational investment vehicle for Singapore – its NWF – to maximize long-term value as an active shareholder of a given portfolio of assets, while GIC was set up as the sovereign wealth fund (SWF), or the fund manager of its cash reserves. The difference between the two is not dissimilar to that between private equity and hedge funds. The investment strategies of private equity firms are geared towards long-term holdings, multiple-year investment strategies in companies, large-scale projects, or other tangibles not easily converted to cash. This includes greater control and influence over operations or asset management to influence long-term returns. Hedge funds usually focus on short- or medium-term liquid securities, which are more quickly convertible to cash, and where they do not have direct control over the business or asset in which they are investing.

The Singapore government is a net creditor, with net assets of some $127 billion, with the combined funds of Temasek and GIC totaling $497 billion – $177 billion and $320 billion respectively. This comfortably exceeds the national public debt of $370 billion, now equal to 111% of GDP. Government debt has an AAA rating and is issued primarily to help develop the country's bond market. In 2013, Singapore was ranked second in the BlackRock Sovereign Risk Index after Norway. Singapore tends to run a fiscal surplus in its national balances. Government reserves enable it to adopt fiscal stimulus measures during business cycle downturns without needing higher taxes. During the 2008–09 global financial crisis, the authorities relied heavily on a countercyclical fiscal policy to bolster growth.

To continue growing, Temasek is compelled to invest internationally either with add-on acquisitions through its portfolio companies, or with new investments. Recent acquisitions indicate a strategic move away from finance, seeming to bet instead on consumer goods and the growth of the emerging Asian middle class. Examples include the acquisition of a 25% stake in AS Watson Group, one of the largest Asian retail health and beauty product groups, and a tender offer worth $4.2 billion for Olam International, the listed, globally integrated soft commodities supply chain manager.[19]

Temasek also recently diversified geographically, including broader investment in Africa. In 2014, it became the largest shareholder in Seven Energy, a Nigeria-based oil and gas group, shortly after buying 20% of several gas fields in Tanzania controlled by London-listed Ophir Energy. In 2011, it founded the investment company Tana Africa Capital on an equal footing with the Oppenheimer family investment vehicle E. Oppenheimer & Son International, to focus on food, retail, and logistics investments on the continent.[20]

Still, more than half of Temasek's portfolio remains in financial services and TMT (see Figure 8.1). Its 10 largest companies represent about 60% of its holdings, while the largest, Singtel, accounted for about 13% of the net portfolio value. Along with China Construction Bank and DBS, with 6 and 5% respectively, these three largest companies totaled 25%.

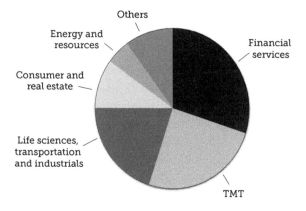

FIGURE 8.1 Temasek's portfolio, by sector, 2014

These investments span countries and regions, with a 55% exposure to the mature economies ranging from Singapore, Japan, South Korea, Australia and New Zealand, to North America and Europe (see Figure 8.2). In the developed economies, Singapore has the largest single exposure, totaling 31%, followed by Australia with 10%. The remaining 45% exposure is in growth regions, primarily in Asia, where China (25% of the total) is the single largest destination, while Latin America, Africa, Central Asia and the Middle East constitute only 3% of NPV.

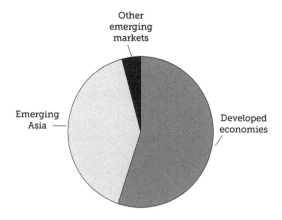

FIGURE 8.2 Temasek's portfolio, by region, 2014

The portfolio has grown from S$354 million ($280 million) at its inception in 1974, with an 18% average annual return in US$, to S$223 billion ($77 billion) today.[21]

Temasek's track record as an investment house is impressive even compared with private sector competitors. Some critics say this warrants skepticism since Singaporean stock returns have averaged less than 8% since 1974.[22] Another study claimed that these returns are still derived primarily from its holdings in local monopolies.[23] Yet, without the professional governance from Temasek, these monopoly rents may have been squandered in organizational inefficiency.

Dividend payments to the government as the sole shareholder in Temasek are part of the Singapore government's investment income. Dividend contributions from Temasek are shared between present and future generations in a formula where at least half the income derived from past reserves must be saved for future generations. The Singapore government may use the remaining income in annual budgetary spending.

Governance in Temasek today

Temasek was incorporated in 1974 under the Singapore Companies Act, making it wholly government-owned through the Ministry of Finance. The country's constitution sets out a framework for safeguarding reserves (net assets), providing for the president to exercise certain powers including appointing directors and the CEO, reviewing its budget and certain proposed transactions. These decisions should be supported through a transparent recommendation from the Council of Advisors to the president and presented to the prime minister and Parliament. Checks and balances are also in place, for example presidential decisions can be overruled by a two-thirds parliamentary majority. The constitution also gives the president ultimate oversight through audited financial statements and an annual procedure to approve whether past government reserves are needed to support Temasek, thereby making transparent any government subsidy to the company[24] and also likely limiting the size of any subsidy.

The company also has clearly defined delegation of responsibilities and accountabilities between levels in the chain of command, with the board assigned overall responsibility for long-term strategic objectives, annual budgets, annual audited statutory accounts, major investment and divestment proposals, major funding proposals, appointing the CEO and succession planning, as well as board changes.

Meanwhile, Temasek's Executive Committee reviews, considers, and approves matters relating to supervision and control, financing and funding proposals, mergers and acquisitions up to a set threshold, changes in shareholding structure, dividend policy, and any other major operational decisions delegated by the board. It has also other specialized committees, including an Audit Committee and a Leadership Development and Compensation Committee.[25]

The holding company charter clearly states its single objective – to maximize value. The charter is a professionally designed document outlining management of investments to create and maximize shareholder value, balancing risks through a risk management framework that covers strategic, performance, and operational risks, including financial risks such as interest rates, foreign currency exposures, and counterparty credit risk. A value at risk (VaR) statistical model is used for portfolio market risk assessment, and monthly stress tests and scenario analyses gauge the effect of low probability, high impact events to complement the VaR model.

Temasek started out with a basic management structure, mainly of former government employees, to handle its shareholding in the, at first, rather eclectic portfolio of companies. It has since improved professionalism, not least through opening the economy up in the early 1990s and is now established as an attractive participant in the commercial sector. With regard to the senior professionals, now more than 40% of management have an international background, including Simon Israel (former Asia Pacific chairman of Danone, the world's largest yogurt maker, and Sara Lee Corp. in Asia), executive director and president, who retired from Temasek in 2011, and Gregory Curl, a former executive at Bank of America, now overseeing its US and financial services holdings. Four out of thirteen nonexecutive directors are international executives, including Marcus Wallenberg, Swedish industrialist, Robert Zoellick, former World Bank president, and Peter Voser, former CEO at Royal Dutch Shell. It has around 490 employees, with 29 different nationalities, in more than 11 cities around the world.

As an active shareholder, it professes not to participate in the day-to-day management of its portfolio companies, a claim legally emphasized by the statement that it does not assume any liability for its financial risks, but holds their respective boards accountable for the financial performance and risk management processes of their companies.[26]

Employees are incentivized through a company bonus system, driven by performance as individuals, as teams, and within the company as a whole. Returns above or below a risk-adjusted threshold determine the incentive pool for long-term incentives, which are paid on top of annual cash bonuses and medium-term incentives.

Transparency is important

Temasek is an exempt private company under the Companies Act and therefore not required by law to file its financial statements with the relevant public registry in Singapore. However, the company has chosen to publish a Group Financial Summary and portfolio performance in the annual Temasek Review since 2004. And the company publishes consolidated financial statements prepared in accordance with Singapore Financial Reporting Standards, which differ somewhat from International Financial Reporting Standards, and in accordance with generally accepted accounting principles in the US. Further, these are audited by international auditing firms.

Thanks to its success and well-organized governance, Temasek has an overall corporate credit rating, independent of the government of Singapore, currently at Aaa (Moody's) and AAA (Standard & Poor's). The company has also issued several bond prospectuses, further increasing transparency while widening the stakeholder base of professional investors scrutinizing Temasek as an investment.

Temasek as a role model

As a pioneering wealth fund with more than 40 years of exceptional financial performance, Temasek has become a role model for a number of countries that have emulated its success, including Malaysia, Vietnam, Abu Dhabi, and Dubai, and European attempts, such as Finland.

Recently, China has officially proclaimed that it intends to improve its state-ownership mechanisms and create a Temasek-like holding company.

Perhaps part of the allure for the Chinese government in learning from the Temasek example is its successful international expansion. Critics would say that it is one thing to manage in an island state with 5 million inhabitants and something else entirely doing so in the world's most populous country, with over 1.35 billion people. Xi Jinping, the current president of China, has probably found encouragement from Sun Tzu, legendary military strategist and author of *The Art of War*, who, to paraphrase, said that commanding a large or small army is just the same, it's all about organization.

For China, emulating Temasek could be a boon. SOEs still account for between one-third and one-quarter of GDP, and expressed as a share of manufacturing, SOEs account for 20% of output. Yet their performance is dismal.[27] State firms' return on assets relative to cost of capital is extremely low (near 3.7% for 2013), less than half the cost of capital. There is an enormous opportunity to boost economic growth in China by restructuring the public asset portfolio, as a part of structural reforms and also to curb corruption and poor asset allocation. The experience of Temasek indicates that consolidating the entire portfolio in an independent holding company ring-fenced from government interference and with professional management would be exactly what China needs.

In Chapter 9, we look more closely at how to take the first crucial step in that direction by making public assets transparent and accountable.

9

Monetizing value improves democracy and yields

One would never expect a politician in charge of healthcare, or their ministry appointees, to run a hospital or decide which X-ray equipment to buy. Yet, as long as the governance of public commercial assets is kept inside government, as in a centrally planned economy, politicians and government bureaucrats will always be suspected of interference. If fear of being accused of interference leads to totally passive ownership, orphaned SOEs may also fail.

In this chapter, we discuss how the governance of SOEs can be made transparent, thereby enabling value creation and, in the end, also promoting sound democratic principles.

The most fundamental issue in any business involves maximizing economic value, which requires skills and experiences that are quite different from those required for political wrangling and compromise. Thus, as we have noted, the worlds of business strategy and political tactics are entirely incompatible, which is why politicians can rarely be ideal business owners. Political concerns are so much broader than just value maximization, and then sometimes much narrower. In the best case, a government seeks to promote wider social aims. But a politician also needs to build coalitions, which may require vagueness and blurred promises. In the worst of cases, selfish aims, clientelism, or simple ignorance dominate.

In contrast, managers and investors, with their expertise in commercial operations, thrive on quantifiable goals that everyone is expected to rally behind to ensure success. They strive for a coherent, well-understood, and clearly communicated culture, with individual initiatives within a defined framework. Also, stock markets and nearly all external financial stakeholders depend on the delivery of well-defined quantifiable promises or objectives.

The divide between political and business competences and culture leaves a vacuum in government-owned companies. In our view, as long as government is involved in any commercial asset, this divide must be bridged by independent, professional governance of these public assets.

Political directives for SOEs to maximize profits will not do the trick. In many cases, SOEs are monopolies, national champions, or favored companies that can use their advantage to rake in excess profits – to the detriment to the country. Rather, in many emerging economies with less developed markets, government holdings are viewed much as the Hindu god Ganesh – the elephant god and remover of obstacles in an otherwise impenetrable environment – able to reap greater profits. As an example, Chinese state-controlled oil and financial institutions have accounted for between three-fifths and four-fifths of all profits made by companies listed on the Chinese stock market since 2005.[1]

Moreover, the public ownership of commercial assets is akin to an addiction, a comforting and convenient habit that can satisfy many vested interests. Although operating the company is a drag on the public budget and the economy, the government and its co-dependents tend to be in denial. For them, avoiding transparency, which would force a closer look at the facts and the reality of the situation, is often the first order of business.

Breaking this addiction begins with asking three questions: What value do the assets have? What do those assets cost taxpayers? How can they be used to obtain more reasonable yields?

Combining active management with political control

An owner wanting to actively take charge of a portfolio can hire professional "corporate governors" to achieve more efficient utilization of their invested capital in an effort to create higher returns by actively developing the portfolio assets. "Active ownership" is what owners, entrepreneurs, and private equity professionals do on a daily basis in the private sector. And governments can hire professionals to manage their portfolio of commercial assets in much the same way as pension funds do when they contract "general partners" when investing in a private equity fund.

Active governance is not simply a question of avoiding waste, corruption, vested interests, and crony capitalism. Active governance also means developing the business and optimizing the capital structure with a competitive operational strategy to maximize value. Doing so with public wealth should aim to yield financial returns similar to comparable assets in the private sector – to benefit all taxpayers. The gap in yield between a publicly owned company and its private competitor is really a loss of income to taxpayers. The loss benefits a vested interest – paid for by taxpayers.

A better focus on the value of public wealth is particularly important as the population ages. Countries need to have stronger balance sheets with good returns on their assets so they can pay for the promises made by the welfare state – for pensions, healthcare, and education, among others.

In the best of worlds, governments act as referees, independent from all participants, aiming to reduce monopoly profits and inefficiency, lowering prices for end-users, increasing investment and productivity, and encouraging competition in the sector. This stance is irreconcilable with direct involvement in public firms. As long as these roles are held within the same government offices, they will burden the government, and the economy.

In his most recent book, Francis Fukuyama discussed his three building blocks necessary for a well-ordered society: a strong state, the rule of law, and democratic accountability. He argues that all three are essential. Moreover, he argues, what matters most is getting the sequence right. Democracy doesn't come first. A strong state does. States that try to democratize before they acquire the capacity to rule effectively invariably fail.[2]

In a similar spirit, we argue that governing public assets in a political process without attention to principles will fail. The most important principles are:

1 *Transparency:* including both transparent asset management and proper accounting, as well as the transparent pursuit of social aims.
2 *Clear objective:* allowing for value maximization as the single objective.
3 *Political independence:* with an independent ownership vehicle operating at arm's length from any governmental function.

These three are intertwined. Political independence without transparency or a clear objective will create a behemoth without any direction or checks and balances. Keeping a clear objective is not possible without transparency brought about by independent valuations and appropriate accounting.

Transparency

Transparency is the essential prerequisite. Without transparency, there is no map, no way to find the assets or the ability to consolidate the portfolio, separating out nonmarket assets. Transparency is the guiding principle in order to measure and assign responsibility and accountability for developing operational efficiency, capital structure, and a competitive business model. Without transparency, vested interests easily invent arguments to maintain the status quo. As long as relevant information about public commercial assets, including their size, value, and yield, is kept from the general public, the more likely it is that these assets will fail to come high on the political agenda. Monetizing public assets makes hidden public wealth transparent, and also strengthens a government's ability to pursue social aims besides value maximization.

Transparency and disclosure are essential components in any modern corporate governance framework. They support efforts to improve the quality and effectiveness of oversight. They include applying international standards for accounting and financial reporting, as well as being subject to annual external audits. All these components expose performance to greater public scrutiny, and, in turn, provide a strong incentive to improve the management, monitoring, and execution of ownership more effectively.

In the case of real estate, transparency would go beyond setting up a government cadaster, and using accrual-based accounting and a balance sheet, as suggested by Buiter[3] and Tanzi and Prakash.[4] Using a holding company would plug into all the related private sector tools and frameworks used on a regular basis for similar assets, such as creating a proper professional inventory of all real estate assets, with independent valuations and the accounting and legal frameworks that come with it. With this institutional platform, we could completely abolish many of the ad hoc solutions that public governance usually involves.

The concept of transparency for a portfolio of publicly owned commercial assets also includes transparently measuring growth (or at least change) and assigning accountability, that is, transparency equal to that of a corporation listed on stock markets, as well as transparently identifying any social objectives being pursued. When governments want SOEs to pursue social aims (in addition to maximizing value), these aims must be made transparent without confusing them with the objective of value maximization. This means SOEs should be explicitly paid for pursuing social aims, or fined for negative externalities, such as monopoly pricing or added environmental burdens.

Implementing a comprehensive transparency policy, such as the Swedish Government Guidelines for External Reporting,[5] should oblige a government to publish a consolidated annual report for all state assets, including real estate. These financial statements should also be audited by an internationally recognized auditing firm. This report should consolidate the annual reports of individual state assets, as well as assets not yet incorporated, such as all the real estate and property, including land and forestry resources. Each annual report would therefore provide a fair picture of the development of the public portfolio, every major holding, its commercial activities, financial position, and bottom line, in accordance with laws and accepted practice. A good example of such transparency can be found in Solidium, Finland's national wealth fund, founded in 2008.[6] Moreover, subsidies should also be separately identified.

Cash flows between government and public holdings should also be transparent, to ensure the efficient use of government funds and enable the assessment of the portfolio's total fiscal risk. Since we know that the fiscal impact of public assets can amount to a significant percentage of GDP, this should include dividend payments, subsidies, or capital injections into failed operations (as with banks or other entities).

The potential for privatization also suffers due to poor financial risk management, as when entities planned for privatization are too heavily burdened with debt, which drives their value so low they cannot be privatized other than to creditors.

Transparency can make a big difference. The business of soccer would likely not be the multi-billion dollar sport it is today without the transparency provided by TV and the Internet, analyzing and scrutinizing every move of every player, every club, and every game.

Clear objective

The second guiding principle, pursuing a clear objective, means embracing, implementing, and communicating value maximization as the sole objective for the public portfolio. A single objective is the prerequisite for any owner in order to align their interest with the company's, from the board, to management and every employee. When the objective is not clear, results tend to be equally unclear and the company will likely lose its way. We see this in *Alice's Adventures in Wonderland*, when Alice asks the Cheshire Cat: "Would you tell me, please, which way I ought to go from here?," only to get the reply: "That depends a good deal on where you want to get to." Her reply: "I don't much care where," prompts the Cat's entirely reasonable response: "Then it doesn't matter which way you go."

But we know that "where you want to go" in business does matter a great deal. What's more, it also matters a great deal who gets there first – as well as who gets there most efficiently. For publicly owned businesses, it is not enough to get "somewhere," as the Cheshire Cat explains, "if you only walk long enough." As we've seen in previous chapters, that can be a huge waste of taxpayer money and, indeed, national wealth.

In working toward value maximization, the business also has the option of introducing incentives to all employees, as some of the Swedish SOEs did (as discussed in Chapter 8).[7]

A clear objective is also fundamental for transparency and oversight. Easily quantifiable targets allow corporate governors to measure performance. Commercial assets also charged with carrying out a public policy objective should publish a clear description of this objective and fully quantify the cost of achieving this policy, whether the costs are covered by subsidies or otherwise, as suggested by the 2005 OECD Guidelines on Corporate Governance of State-owned Enterprises.[8]

Publicly owned institutions have an inherent advantage over private companies in some markets, not the least in financial services. Governments have sometimes addressed this effectively, as when the UK government published a code of conduct to demonstrate that it would not use its ownership status in Northern Rock (the "good bank" remnant of Northern Rock Building Society nationalized early in the global financial crisis) to an unfair competitive advantage in gathering deposits. In other cases, as in the US bailout of AIG, there were no such controls in place. Competitors therefore felt AIG was able to use its government ownership as an unfair competitive weapon.

The EU has detailed and complex regulations restricting state aid. But these seem to be honored as much in the breach as in the observance, apparently based on the country concerned and the number of national jobs at stake. The precise outcome of state aid negotiations will depend on the economic pros and cons involved in each circumstance and, naturally, on political horse-trading. Open and fair competition, with the government acting as an impartial regulator (advocating the consumer perspective), is the basis on which any sector can thrive. Also, any asset must transparently disclose all the support they receive from their owner.

Political independence

Political independence is necessary to ensure a level playing field and avoid market distortions where state-owned commercial assets and private sector companies compete. But political independence works in both directions. It also protects politicians from becoming embroiled in corporate troubles, and from temptation of clientelism or even corruption.

The legal and regulatory framework for state-owned assets should include a clear separation between the government ownership governance function and other policy functions, in particular with regard to market regulations. This kind of institutional reform enables a transparent separation between commercial objectives and nonmarket-oriented objectives, and creates a distinct separation between commercial assets and nonmarket assets from an operational and organizational perspective.

Implementing separation of this kind is an important, fundamental political decision, as the two different types of assets require completely different modes of governance and management capabilities. Nonmarket assets, used to carry out government policy, should therefore be governed by the same framework as any government policy. These can be managed by civil servants within the governmental framework, and require the relevant experience. Meanwhile, commercial assets, as the name implies, should be governed within a framework and management structure similar to private sector competitors.

Once separated from political control, the managers of a commercial assets portfolio should be on track to adopt a more professional approach, which should, in turn, enable them to close any performance gap with their private sector peers. The challenge can be outlined in the publication of a financial report of the entire portfolio. This should show the total value, yield, and key financial data for the portfolio as a whole, and include a breakdown of its major sectors to publicly state the portfolio's character and the challenges or environment each asset faces.

Companies can be run commercially even when receiving governmental subsidies, as when rail or bus services allow free or reduced rate travel for pensioners, or for postal services to rural or sparsely populated areas. These should be subject to competitive public tender processes to ensure cost efficiency. The important factors here involve ensuring a transparent, formalized understanding of the nature and cost of any subsidy, and preferably exposing the achievement of social aims to competition through some kind of public procurement.

Political independence is not always achieved by creating a formally independent holding company. In most countries, there are informal ties and dependencies that create problems. Several steps can strengthen political independence.

Broadening the stakeholder base by raising debt based on an independent credit rating for the holding company provides an additional level of political independence, as this measures stand-alone credit risk. Some one-third of NWFs have a credit rating. For example, Temasek in Singapore has a rating independent from the government, while the credit rating for Mubadala, in Abu Dhabi, is backed by the government. Independence of this kind is still debatable and will remain so until tested properly. Nevertheless, the procedures involved in obtaining a credit rating provide a test for the company, as well as valuable information to the market. Also, the constant effort to maintain or improve a rating will inevitably strengthen the holding company's independence further.

Listing the holding company on a stock market is, of course, the most powerful way of broadening the stakeholder base, increasing transparency and market pressure on the equity. To date, only CITIC in China is still a listed vehicle (in Hong Kong). The Romanian state holding company, Fondul Proprietatea, created to compensate citizens for property confiscated under the former communist dictatorship, was listed in 2011. Here, though, the government has slowly sold all its shares, so the company is now fully private. Before privatizing it, the Romanian government introduced another first in managing public wealth – outsourcing the management of the holding company and its portfolio to US-based asset managers Franklin Templeton Investments. This is undoubtedly a good way to demonstrate arm's length holding by the government in obtaining management of the portfolio through a competitive public process.

Breaking the addiction

Much like gaining trust, political independence is difficult to achieve. It takes self-discipline even to establish an image of independence from political control. And even after a great deal of effort, one small misstep can quickly cause the public and stakeholders to lose all confidence that the government or its representatives have truly abandoned short-term political interference.

Developed and emerging economies alike must address their addiction to public ownership of significant assets. Western, developed countries need to change because they are going broke and cannot afford to ignore this idle resource on their balance sheets. The economies of the emerging world need to reassess their view of public assets in order to improve economic growth, as argued by Micklethwait and Wooldridge in their recent book, *The Fourth Revolution: The Global Race to Reinvent the State.*[9] The age of smart government has begun and it seems the west is being left behind in this race. The most advanced governments in the field of managing public wealth do not include the US, but are found in Asia and, to a limited extent, Europe. The driving factor here is that these countries, perhaps due to their size, have acknowledged it is a race.

Moving to the professional management of public assets means making an active decision. But this is often triggered by a harsh awakening in the midst of a crisis that enables the mobilization of considerable political will, prepared to meet head on the vested interests directly benefitting from the assets. When discussing the malign effects of interest group politics on economic growth and democracy, economist Mancur Olson argued that it would take a war or a revolution to stop unproductive and costly rent seeking by vested interests.[10]

This is perhaps why when the Thatcher government initiated reforms in 1979 in response the prolonged UK crisis of the 1970s, it was seen as the undisputed champion in this – hence "Thatcherism." The UK no doubt succeeded in revitalizing its economy thanks to the huge wave of structural reforms and privatizations carried out in the 1980s and 90s. But equal credit should be given to the existence of a strong state, markets that were still functioning (including financial markets), and a well-developed civil society able to digest such massive transformation.

We argue that even well-developed economies, such as the UK, can benefit hugely from institutionalizing such a transition even more transparently, separating ownership from governmental regulatory responsibility more clearly. Independent institutions with a clear objective help focus the debate on outcomes, such as the actual service and product provided.

Given that the bulk of wealth is owned by local governments, a country would benefit from vesting its public commercial assets into an NWF not only at central government level, but also a separate holding company or "local" wealth fund for the local government level.

The state holding companies in Asia are often instruments of state capitalism – not entirely dissimilar to the old East India Company – enthusiastic globalizers, venturing abroad partly as money-making organizations and partly as quasi-official agents of their home governments. Many are not only keen on getting their governments to provide soft loans and diplomatic muscle, but also on building infrastructure – roads, hospitals, and schools – in return for guaranteed access to raw materials.[11]

The European NWFs in Austria and Finland adopted the professional holding company model for more defensive purposes to get their portfolio into a better shape as a vehicle of development, preventing vital state assets from being taken over by foreign instruments of state or crony capitalism.

In Chapters 10–13, we look more closely at how current NWFs operate, and how they could operate in many more countries.

10

The transition to national wealth funds

Historically, countries have managed their public assets in a fragmented way depending on the nature of the assets or their history. Typically, railways, telecommunications, and other similar assets were controlled through, for example, the ministry of transportation/communication, and electricity assets through the ministry of energy and so on. This structure was natural in a centrally planned economy and a market economy when the regulation of a sector and the ownership of the state monopoly assets in the same sector was integrated under the same line ministry.

Moving from this structure toward outsourcing governance to an independent institutional framework, a holding company operating at arm's length from politics – the national wealth fund (NWF) – enables the use of the appropriate private sector toolkit. However, for most governments, the road to this goal is not straightforward, but full of challenges, and choices between political survival and economic sense.

We define a national wealth fund as a ring-fenced holding company at arm's length from short-term political influence by the government, while a regional wealth fund or urban wealth fund operates at a regional and local level (see Figure 10.1).

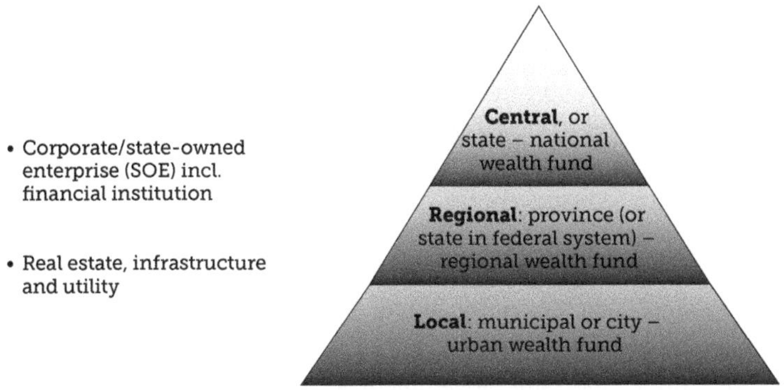

- Corporate/state-owned enterprise (SOE) incl. financial institution

- Real estate, infrastructure and utility

Central, or state – national wealth fund

Regional: province (or state in federal system) – regional wealth fund

Local: municipal or city – urban wealth fund

FIGURE 10.1 Wealth funds illustrated

Such funds are set up to achieve the operational requirements, which Buiter (1983) and Tanzi and Prakash (2000) have argued for, needed to manage these assets more efficiently. It would conform to the legal framework that all private sector commercial assets are subject to, including a national register/cadaster and International Financial Reporting Standards accounting that would produce market values of the portfolio, which could help determine alternative uses of each asset and thereby efficient management.

First, we consider how public assets often have been governed. This sets the stage for our detailed description of the transition to NWFs.

Traditional decentralized governance

The decentralized structure integrating the regulatory function and governance of SOEs in government ministries followed historical precedent. The financial perspective on the governance of commercial assets was absent, partly because assets were not seen or defined as commercial. Corporate governance and the management of the ownership of state commercial assets should be understood in the classic definition: "the ways in which suppliers of finance to corporations assure themselves of getting a return on their investment."[1] Lately, the definition has become broader, as expressed by the Global Corporate Governance Forum: "Corporate governance refers to the structures and processes for the direction and control of companies. Corporate governance concerns the relationships among the management, Board of Directors, controlling shareholders, minority shareholders and other stakeholders," which is an adaptation of the definition in the 1992 UK Cadbury Code.[2]

After waves of deregulation, the commercial aspect of public assets became more apparent, but this also exposed inherent conflicts. The idea of self-regulation within a ministry, combining two irreconcilable objectives such as regulation and ownership under the same roof, is often likened to a judicial system where the chief justice and the chief of police would be governed under the same government agency, or a game of football where the referee would also be playing in one of the teams. Such a conflict of interest, often within a complex web of overlapping, sometimes contradictory legislation, creates a nontransparent governance vacuum, and vast opportunities for vested interests.

The completely decentralized model has largely been abandoned in the western world and only prevails in a few economies such as Ukraine and Greece.

Technological development, such as the Internet, mobile telephony, and logistics, and an increasingly globalized world economy made many business models obsolete. Improved operational and financial efficiency required radical restructurings with risk attached that would be better managed by the private sector if privatized. In this environment, government-owned commercial assets are a mixed blessing. Regardless of how large or small the government's shareholding in a company is, it will always be considered a government-owned company in times of trouble. A politician responsible for the ownership of a commercial asset is, sooner or later, caught between a rock and a hard place. At some point, a difficult choice has to be made such as between maximizing the number of employees and salary levels or maximizing profits and value in the company. Politicians may shy away from making decisions on a strictly commercial basis, such as closing factories or reducing employment opportunities, if it risks their popular appeal.

A dual command structure was sometimes introduced as a half-measure to placate the growing requirements from international investors and capital markets, whereby the ministry of finance comes in as a partnering ministry, alongside the line ministry. The ministry of finance was meant to have a special focus on financial and fiscal monitoring, almost like a public CFO. It was seen as a step toward modernizing the institutional framework that was managing state assets, introducing a more financial approach, including a single objective of value maximization, and thereby a somewhat better oversight function.

It is essential for governments to be able to assess the fiscal risk associated with the ownership of commercial assets, as outlined by the World Bank in its framework to assess risk of state bodies.[3] This includes the risk of unexpected budgetary funding calls to resolve liquidity or solvency issues, or to make up for shortfalls on promised dividends that have been budgeted on the revenue side. Further, the government needs to understand debt levels and levels of outstanding guarantees. This can amount to substantial sums, as with the explosion in borrowing by SOEs and local governments that has pushed China's debt-to-GDP ratio to 251% in mid-2014, from 147% before the financial crisis.[4]

The ministry of finance is ultimately responsibility for financial and fiscal management. Therefore, a line ministry would have to share the required information with the ministry of finance. Yet, dual command is never ideal. The reluctance to avoid assigning clear responsibility and accountability allows vested interests to fill the void and control the entire value chain – as in the proverb, where two people fight, the third wins (taking all the spoils).

This is also the case when a specialized governmental privatization agency is formed, ostensibly to manage the privatization of assets. Such an agency may act as some kind of in-house corporate financial adviser, as in Greece and Ukraine. But, without the legal transfer of ownership rights, this simply adds another layer of governmental oversight, ripe with opportunities for conflicting interests to take over rather than a focused approach where accountability is clearly assigned to a single corporate institution, its board, and an individual chairman and chief executive.

Difficulties in persuading line ministries to relinquish ownership of publicly owned assets is often cited as the main reason why governments and/or well-meaning prime ministers fail to fully consolidate a public portfolio under a single unit. In countries with a stronger state, less dependent on vested interests, a specific opportunity may arise in a crisis or when a ministerial appointment can be conditional on removing the commercial assets prior to the appointment. However, once the appointment has been made, little bargaining leverage remains for a government leader to pursue consolidation.

As discussed in Chapter 8, consolidation in Sweden was made possible by merging several ministries with large commercial holdings into a single super ministry, agreed among senior Social Democrats before the 1998 election. In comparison, a similar consolidation of SOEs in Finland took more than five years of political deliberations and parliamentary reports. Other countries do not even contemplate this kind of transition until a financial crisis erupts, requiring an immediate improvement in the utilization of state resources.

A consolidated model: toward creating a holding company

Despite the challenges, more governments are gradually moving toward consolidating the management of ownership rights and the financial monitoring of SOEs into a single owner/management entity, as recommended by the OECD.[5]

The vehicles consolidated in this way were set up either as a separate government entity, or as an independent ring-fenced holding company that maintains an arm's length relationship with the government – a national wealth fund (NWF). So far, these NWFs have been set up mainly to manage corporate assets at the central government level, while some countries have also consolidated the governance of some of their real estate assets in ring-fenced independent holding companies, such as Bundesimmobiliengesellschaft in Austria. On the other hand, Sweden, and other countries, opted for a segmented approach and created a number of specialist real estate companies, such as Vasakronan (office and commercial properties), Jernhusen (railway-related properties), and Akademiska Hus (properties related to universities and higher education).

A holding company is already the preferred model for temporary restructuring programs for other government-owned assets. When faced with a financial crisis, most governments tend to recognize the benefits of outsourcing the management of commercial assets to a private sector holding company in order to fully develop the value of these assets.

This is exemplified by the bad bank concept, where nonperforming assets are taken over from an ailing bank or banking system – first used in the US for the S&L crisis of the late 1970s and 1980s (see Chapter 3) and used in Europe and Asia in the decades since. Several large public asset restructuring and privatization programs were also carried out using the independent holding company model, including in post-reunification Germany, which formed Treuhandanstalt to privatize the vast portfolio of the former East German state assets.

The Italian government used a holding company version during the Depression in 1933. It set up IRI as a combined bad bank/development vehicle. However, in the economic build-up after World War II, the lack of political independence quickly turned it into a tool for state intervention and state capitalism, soon growing into one the largest state-owned conglomerates in the world. Ultimately, its assets were privatized and the holding company dissolved. Today, Fintecna, a holding company controlled by the Ministry of Economy and Finance via Cassa Depositi e Prestiti, manages the few remaining assets from IRI, such as Fincantieri, with the remaining mandate to support government privatizations and restructurings.

In less turbulent times, politicians often opt for the in-house government entity rather than relinquishing direct control to an independent holding company. This is partially explained by the desire to retain the ability to create or solidify alliances through appointing cronies as directors of these companies. This also happens in the private sector, famously exemplified by the board of Disney under its CEO Michael Eisner (in post 1984–2005), which included the former headmistress of his children's school and the designer of his house.

Another frequent argument against consolidating assets, as we propose it, is the deeply ingrained fear in some cultures of delegating so much economic power to a single entity or individual. The counterarguments to this include noting the concentration of power most countries have vested in their defense, police, and judicial systems, as well as an independent central bank.

In countries with weaker central governments and significant crony capitalism, the fear of consolidating state-owned commercial assets under a single holding company with a single CEO is that it could then fall under the control of local oligarchs or be taken out of the country. However, the possibility of a fragmented portfolio, lacking transparency and state-of-the-art governance, coming under the control of various oligarchs is probably even higher. As an example, due to its fragmented nature and the lack of transparency, government-owned real estate has a tendency to "disappear" in many countries that lack a proper accounting system and a central registry enabling the professional management of commercial real estate.

Moreover, the very act of consolidation and the imposition of a clear objective and greater transparency are the most important of (many) steps necessary to strengthen central government influence in society against these forces. Vested interests will likely not give up their source of power and revenues without a struggle.

The government entity approach

Consolidation can improve the government's capacity for asset governance even more if the assets are managed by a separate entity within government. This would constitute a significant improvement in transparency. This approach means establishing a dedicated unit, often within the ministry of finance or ministry of industry, as in Sweden, Norway, and the UK. Alternatively, this could be set up as a special unit or ministry reporting directly to the prime minister's office, as in Finland and China.

Ultimately, commercial assets can never be fully developed inside a government bureaucracy, due to the many contradictions and irreconcilable objectives between business and politics. Government-owned commercial assets should be subject to the same legal framework as their private sector equivalents, and function under the same conditions. This allows the public assets to compete with the private sector on a more equal basis. As discussed above, transferring real estate assets to a private sector vehicle would give the government the tools to make optimal use of these assets, based on full information and with the incentives to make good decisions.

A clear commercial mandate and a professional ownership institution further add to political independence. Historically, in many well-documented cases, the boards of publicly owned companies have been weak, and political interference in daily management issues is the rule rather than the exception.[6]

Culturally and organizationally, the difference between politics and business cannot be underestimated. The political process applies a top-down approach, with parliament or government issuing decisions that are implemented through a bureaucratic apparatus. The government minister has sole responsibility, using their ministry largely as support staff. Successful commercial decisions rely on delegating responsibility and accountability in order to allow speedy responses. In the commercial world and in mature markets with established products, it is the salesperson, not the chief executive, who is, in effect, the front person, with the organization there to support the sales effort. These opposite approaches inevitably clash.

Finally, the ability of a government to pay the market rate for the necessary sector and business expertise is a limiting factor in developing a fully professional ownership unit within the confines of government offices. Built-in legal constraints prevent government administrations from assuming full commercial responsibility for managing commercial assets.

The national wealth fund approach

Putting state-owned commercial assets into an independent ring-fenced holding company at arm's length from short-term political interference and with professional management brings strategic and financial expertise and advantages to the operations, as well as economic benefits to the country.

But commonly, professional management of public assets meets resistance. Taking another sports analogy, this kind of resistance to professionalism shows similarities with the historical resistance seen against professional sports. The upper classes long held amateurism in sports as the ideal. But this ideal faced steady erosion in the 20th century with the growth and enthusiastic acceptance of many professional sports leagues. And finally, by the early 21st century, even the Olympic Games had accepted many professional team sports competitors. Historically, the middle- and upper-class men who dominated the sporting establishment had a self-interest in blocking professionalization in their sport, as this threatened to make it possible for the working classes to compete successfully. Also, working-class men (and the few women) normally worked six days a week, and with Sundays restricted for religious reasons as the day of rest, they had little time for practicing. Today's professional sports, clubs and tournaments have taken most sports to a new level of achievement, creating new industries, as well as allowing countless young people a livelihood they previously could never have dreamed of in and around sports.

The NWF uses all the appropriate private sector tools and institutional frameworks that enable the government to consider the portfolio of commercial assets as a whole from the perspective of operating income and liabilities without any of the constraints of a public sector bureaucracy. Consolidation under a private sector vehicle allows the government to establish strategies for handling lossmaking assets, while the priority of improving performance provides greater opportunities to raise financing and choose optimal circumstances for disposals, in the same way as a private sector owner.

The idea of a government governing assets outside the government bureaucracy is not entirely new. Possibly the first external or "outsourced" public asset governance company the world saw was CDC (Caisse des Dépôts et Consignations, the Deposits and Consignments Fund) in France, which was established in 1816 to restore confidence following the Napoleonic Wars. Its primary mission was, and still is, long-term investment to promote economic development in France, managing savings, retirement pensions, and financing for social housing, education, and social security.

An early example in the US was the depression-era Reconstruction Finance Corporation (RFC), which was set up in 1933 to boost national confidence and help banks restart lending amid the Great Depression. It was modeled on the War Finance Corporation, which had been created to provide financial support to industries and banks essential for the US effort in World War I. After World War II, governments across Europe created special entities to manage state assets and/or fulfill economic developmental objectives. An early example is the German developmental institution KfW (formerly KfW Bankengruppen), established in 1948.

The various types of assets that managers have to deal with have several specific problems, such as capital market inefficiencies, failure to support important economic sectors, such as small and medium-sized enterprises (SMEs), or supporting a distressed banking sector. The wide range of functions, styles, and objectives make precise categorization difficult, but in order to give the context in which the NWF fits into this ecosystem of external managers, we identify four broad categories, which are briefly defined here:

1 *Economic development:* This includes development banks and similar institutions that provide liquidity to national economies, which are involved in long-term lending and investment for projects and companies important to national economic and social development. These institutions have often become substantial owners of domestic assets, often with a focus on SMEs, export promotion, or developing promising sectors, such as FSI (Fonds Stratégique d'Investissement) in France. They sometimes have a role in municipal financing, as, for example, KfW in Germany, CDP in Italy, VEB in Russia, and Bpifrance (the public investment bank, which, in 2013, merged Oséo, CDC Enterprises, and FSI) in France.

2 *Distressed assets:* Several agencies have been set up in the wake of financial crises over the years with the express purpose of holding distressed assets, primarily from the banking sector. In the US, the RFC was created in the Great Depression of the 1930s, followed by the Resolution Trust Corporation in the 1980s after the S&L crisis (as discussed above), and, most recently, the Troubled Asset Relief Program was set up in 2008 during the global financial crisis. In Europe, IRI was set up in Italy during the Great Depression, Securum in Sweden in 1992 during its financial crisis in the early 1990s, and Danaharta in Malaysia after the 1997 Asian financial crisis. More recently, the National Asset Management Agency was established in Ireland in 2009, UK Financial Investments in the UK in 2008, the Hellenic Financial Stability Fund was founded in Greece in 2010, and the Bank Assets Management Company in Slovenia in 2013, all as a response to the global financial crisis.

3 *Privatization:* Some agencies are established primarily for the purpose of privatizing state assets in order to streamline public administration; one of the most ambitious examples being Treuhandanstalt, set up to

manage the privatization of East German assets after German unification in 1990. Others provide central corporate finance services, along with restructuring and privatization expertise. Ownership is rarely transferred to the agency, but is primarily limited to a supervisory role, focusing on assets due for privatization, and rarely on developing the assets of the portfolio. Examples include the Shareholder Executive in the UK, the Hellenic Republic Asset Development Fund in Greece, and the State Property Fund in Ukraine. Fintecna in Italy, created to manage the last parts of IRI, has a somewhat broader mandate but with the ultimate aim of privatization or liquidation.

4 *Wealth management:* Wealth management outsourced to external vehicles can be divided into two broad categories: the management of liquidity, that is, its cash reserves, and managing a government's operational assets such as real estate and corporates.

The traditional management of liquidity reserves (with a view to optimize the balance between risk and return of a government's budgetary surplus within a dedicated entity) has been around for more than a century. The term "sovereign wealth fund" (SWF) was coined as recently as 2005.[7] However, the first examples of what we now know as SWFs were established by individual states in the US in the mid-19th century, designed to fund specific public services.[8] The first sovereign state to establish its own investment fund was Kuwait in 1953, which established the Kuwait Investment Authority for its vast oil revenues. Since 2000, the number of sovereign wealth funds has increased dramatically, reaching a combined market value of almost $7 trillion in 2014.[9]

The difference between the concepts of NWF and SWF is not dissimilar to the difference between private equity funds and hedge funds. Investment strategies in private equity firms are geared towards long-hold, multi-year investment strategies in going concerns and large-scale projects, or other tangibles that are not easily converted to cash. Here, fund managers take greater control and actively influence operations and the development of assets or asset management to generate greater long-term returns. Hedge funds, on the other hand, usually focus on short- or medium-term liquid securities, which can be quickly converted to cash, and where they have no direct control of the business or asset in which they are investing. While Temasek is an example of an NWF, the GIC in Singapore, which acts as the country's fund manager of reserve liquidity, is a clear example of an SWF.

National vs sovereign wealth fund

A *sovereign wealth fund* (SWF) is primarily a fund manager, concerned with managing reserve liquidity, typically investing in securities traded on major mature markets. SWFs are designed to optimize a portfolio through continual securities trading to achieve balance between risk and returns. An example is GIC of Singapore.

A *national wealth fund* (NWF) is an asset manager, concerned with active management of operational assets as a portfolio. The purpose here is to maximize the portfolio value through active management including the development, restructuring and monetization of the individual assets. An example is Temasek of Singapore.

Table 10.1 illustrates the diversity of NWFs. Our selection does not purport to be comprehensive and some have been overlooked or purposely excluded. There are a number of private equity-like institutions in the public sector, such as the Commonwealth Development Corporation in the UK, which we have excluded because they have characteristics related to promoting overseas aid rather than domestic asset management. There are also a number of former public sector agencies, which have moved into the private sector, such as the UK's Industrial and Commercial Finance Corporation, which evolved into 3i, the large listed private equity evergreen funds business. According to Musacchio et al. (2015), in South America, three countries – Peru, Chile, and Bolivia – have what is regarded as holding companies that manage a diversified set of commercial SOEs for the government. However, only FONAFE in Peru would be described as a ring-fenced, incorporated holding company at arm's length from short-term political influence. Hopefully, these examples provide a reasonable cross-section in terms of the styles and functions such institutions can have.

TABLE 10.1 National wealth funds

Name	Country	Operations	Est.	Assets (US$bn)	Sectors
Europe				52	
ÖIAG (Österreichische Industrieholding)	Austria	Holding company and privatization vehicle. Dates back to 1946, with the purpose of protecting Austrian industry from being taken over by the occupying Soviet forces. No credit rating	1967	7	Energy, telecoms, post, mining and steel etc.
Solidium	Finland	Holding company for government shares in listed companies of national interest. Borrows on the capital market but does not have a rating	2008	11	Real estate, forestry, telecoms, steel, etc.
The Hungarian National Asset Management Inc.	Hungary	Holding company for central government owned assets. Previous privatization role replaced by long-term supervision. No credit rating	1991	3	Transport/infrastructure, electricity, water utilities, postal services, agriculture, lottery
Parpublica	Portugal	Holding company for a limited number of assets with a mandate to also manage and restructure assets marked for privatization, as well as acting as adviser to the Ministry of Finance on the remaining portfolio of public assets held directly by the state. Long-term rating Ba3 by Moody's	2000	18	Real estate, construction, water, transport (airport, airline), agriculture/forestry, energy
Rostec Corporation	Russia	Holding company to more than 600 entities held via 13 subholding companies, 8 in the defense and 5 in the civilian sectors, including Kalishnikov, the producer of the ubiquitous machine gun. No credit rating	2007	n.a.	Automotive, aerospace, ordnance, electronics, telecoms, medical technology, etc.

TABLE 10.1 continued

Name	Country	Operations	Est.	Assets (US$bn)	Sectors
SEPI (Sociedad Estatal de Participaciones Industriales)	Spain	Holding company set up to restructure assets previously held by Instituto Nacional de Industria and Instituto Nacional de Hidrocarburos, including 19 majority owned and 7 minority owned companies, as well as indirect shareholdings in some 100 other companies. No credit rating	1995	13	Transportation, mining, defense, energy, food, financials
Americas				24	
FONAFE	Peru	State holding company, acting as owner, manager and privatizer/liquidator for several banks and SOEs. The recovered assets of the banks are still under management. No credit rating	1999	24	Electricity, finance, oil/gas, infrastructure, sewage, others
East Asia				764	
CITIC	China	Potentially a listed state holding company. Originally established to introduce international technolgies and businesses to China. Long-term rating of Ba2 and BB from Moody's and S&P respectively	1979	48	Real estate, construction, financial services, energy, resources, IT, etc
Central Huijin Investment	China	State holding company, wholly owned through CIC, the SWF, to manage the government's holdings (together with the Ministry of Finance) in the main state-owned banks and other financial institutions. No credit rating	2002	397	Financial institutions
SIG (Shanghai International Group)	China	Municipality-owned holding company with three major functions; investment holding, capital operation, and state-owned assets management. No credit rating	2000	22	Financials, infrastructure, real estate, hospitality, etc.

TABLE 10.1 continued

Name	Country	Operations	Est.	Assets (US$bn)	Sectors
Samruk-Kazyna	Kazakhstan	Holding company set to manage the shares of state-owned development institutions, companies and other legal entities. Long-term rating of BBB+ from Fitch and S&P	2008	78	Oil/gas power, financials, energy, metallurgy, chemistry, infrastructure
Khazanah Nasional	Malaysia	Holding company to manage some 50 commercial assets in Malaysia and abroad, reporting to the Ministry of Finance. Long-term rating A3 from Moody's	1965	41	Finance, telecoms, utilities, communication services, IT, transportation
Temasek	Singapore	Holding company originally founded to manage the domestic state-owned commercial assets, which today has expanded internationally with some 30% of its assets in Singapore and the rest internationally. Long-term rating from S&P and Moody's of AAA and Aaa	1974	177	Financial services, telecoms, media/technology, transportation, industrials, life sciences, consumer and real estate, energy, resources
SCIC (State Capital Investment Corporation)	Vietnam	Holding company managing a portfolio of over 500 enterprises and acting as the government privatization vehicle. No credit rating	2005	1	Financial services, energy, manufacturing, telecoms, transportation, consumer products, healthcare, IT
MENA				232	
Mubadala	Abu Dhabi	Holding company with the aim to develop and diversify the economy, through active management of controlling stakes and projects. Long-term ratings from Moody's, Fitch and S&P of Aa3/AA/AA, respectively	2002	61	Energy, aerospace, real estate, healthcare, technology, other
Senaat	Abu Dhabi	Holding company focused on capital-intensive assets. Formerly known as the General Holding Company. No credit rating	1979	7	Metals, oil/gas services, construction/building materials, food/beverages manufacturing

TABLE 10.1 continued

Name	Country	Operations	Est.	Assets (US$bn)	Sectors
Mumtalakat	Bahrain	Holding company for non-gas sector companies, with the aim to create a well-diversified and balanced portfolio across asset classes and geographies. Long-term ratings BBB from Fitch and S&P	2006	11	Financials, telecoms, real estate, tourism, transportation, airlines, food production
Investment Corporation of Dubai	Dubai	Holding company managing a portfolio of state commercial companies, including Emirates Airline, ENOC, Borse Dubai, Emaar Properties etc. No credit rating	2006	70	Financials, transportation, energy, industrials, real estate
Dubai World	Dubai	Holding company with the aim of making Dubai the leading hub for trade and commerce. Holdings include Dubai Ports, Drydocks World, and Istithmar World. No credit rating	2003	10	Shipping, industrials, real estate, entertainment and other
Dubai Holding	Dubai	Holding company established to consolidate the management of large-scale infrastructure and investment projects. Previous long-term rating from Fitch and Moody's of B and B1 respectively, but did not renew its contracts for 2014	2004	31	Telecoms, real estate, financial services, hospitality, healthcare, energy, etc.
Qatari Diar	Qatar	Holding company owned through the Qatar Investment Authority, with local and international assets. Long-term rating of Aa2 and AA from Moody's and S&P respectively	2005	42	Real estate, infrastructure

To date, we have found 16 countries with 21 NWFs, with an aggregate value of some US$1.1 trillion. In value terms, this is only a small fraction (2%) of public commercial assets owned at the central government level, and even less as a share of total public assets. The majority, more than 90%, of the existing NWFs are in Asia, split between the Middle East and North Africa (MENA) and East Asia, and only 7%, in value terms, in Europe and the Americas (see Figure 10.2). Specifically, only 5 out of 34 OECD countries have an NWF to manage their commercial assets, all in Europe and none in the US or Canada. In South America, Peru is considered having a holding company that could be seen as an NWF.

Only Asia has something that could be likened to an NWF on a local level – an "urban wealth fund" – the Shanghai International Group (SIG), Shanghai probably being one of the first cities to have set up a ring-fenced holding company for its commercial assets. Many cities worldwide have public corporates that own commercial activities such as water utilities, but in general these have no ambition to be politically independent or transparent. Often, they are set up as separate entities only for tax purposes.

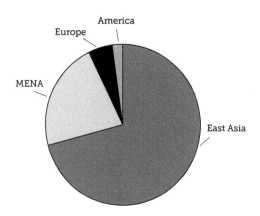

FIGURE 10.2 Geographical distribution of NWFs, in value terms

CITIC in China is unique, being the only NWF potentially listed on the stock exchange and with an international debt rating. Previously, Romania had a listed NWF that has now been fully privatized. Otherwise, ÖIAG in Austria and Solidium in Finland stand out as being relatively more independent, with independent supervisory boards and management.[10] In the case of Solidium, however, there have been allegations that business decisions are influenced by political considerations. In fact, some of Finland's political parties strive for more political control of Solidium, which prompted Alexander Stubb, prime minister of Finland, to say:

> I believe it would be most useful for politicians to keep their hands off Solidium. There's no point in meddling in a business whose goal is to safeguard strategic Finnish ownership and to increase profits – so politicians are involved in some way.[11]

The general idea of a government outsourcing the management of its commercial assets to an external asset management structure is to have access to the entire register of tools and incentive systems available to the private sector, so as to be able to achieve similar yields as if privately held but without giving up control. Consequently, the NWF has borrowed the incorporated holding company model as its preferred institutional framework.

Most existing NWFs have more or less clearly expressed value maximization as their main objectives. One-third of all NWFs have a credit rating from one of the three main rating agencies, borrowing on the back of its balance sheet, although most NWFs do so with the explicit or implicit guarantee of the government. Few have made the effort of Temasek and the Singapore government to clearly express the independence of its debt issuance.

Apart from Solidium, ÖIAG, and, to some extent, Temasek, only a very few have achieved a relevant level of transparency such as publishing a consolidated annual report.

Most of the NWFs do not make further efforts to strengthen political independence beyond setting up a holding company, such as a transparent, professional board nomination process and so on, apart from Solidium, ÖIAG, and, to some extent, Temasek and CITIC (which stands out as the only listed NWF).

With the vast majority of all public assets being hidden under the surface, there is an enormous potential for economic growth in developing these assets in a more commercial environment, if only more countries would set up NWFs and move all central government-owned commercial assets, including real estate, into them. For example, an NWF incorporating all the commercial assets owned by the US federal government alone would most likely be several times the size (in value terms) of the all world's SWFs put together. Improving the yield of these assets would not only save huge amounts of money but also generate an income for the government that could be used to lower taxes, reduce debt, or pay for much needed infrastructure investments.

Consolidating all assets into an NWF: strategy, risk, and reward

The NWF could be the professional steward of a nation's public assets, charged with developing and managing all these assets in a way that maximizes long-term economic value consistent with the principles of corporate governance. The asset class missing in all currently existing NWFs is state-owned real estate. This is most often the largest segment of all public assets. Furthermore, the lion's share of public commercial assets are owned at the local and regional level. Consolidating these public commercial assets, most likely several times the size of what the central government owns, at a local and regional level would require a separate NWF at these respective levels, or rather regional/state and urban wealth fund.

The economic benefits of consolidating all commercial assets into a single company stem from the ability to structure an integrated business plan for the entire portfolio, without constraints on necessary actions to maximize value. This has important scale effects, with lower transaction and operational costs and enables the portfolio to be developed and privatized more efficiently, including the ability to create a segmented approach with identifiable risk profile and the opportunity to merge related assets to create attractive investment profiles.

The financial benefits of consolidating all assets into a single company are the creation of a single vehicle with genuine diversity and scale, allowing the spreading of cash flow over time and thereby more efficient financing of those assets. It could also be a vehicle for improving access or the cost of borrowing on the international capital markets for financing infrastructure projects or other commercial ventures or assets.

While it is difficult to compare performance, controlling for all background factors, some of the NWFs have impressive records. Temasek has a track record as an investment house that would be impressive compared to any private sector competitor, reporting an average annual return of 18% over the 35 years since inception.

In Austria, ÖIAG is a state holding company for seven large firms that comprise one-fourth of the Austrian stock exchange. The holding company has the mandate to privatize parts or all of these firms, or initiate other structural transactions. For example, the telephone company Telekom Austria has been floated and only 28% remains in government ownership. ÖIAG was founded in 1946 in order to quickly nationalize much of Austrian industry to pre-empt an (failed) attempted takeover by the then Soviet occupational forces. In the 1970s, the portfolio had mounting losses, often due to political interference. This led to conversion into an independent stock company, with no politicians at all on its board. ÖIAG now earns healthy returns and has been able to repay the large loans that were accumulated in earlier periods.

When contemplating setting up an NWF, politicians are often tempted to create several holding companies at a national level instead of just one, as can be seen in the Gulf States, and to some extent in China. From a market and operational perspective, it is preferable to resist such fragmentation in order to minimize operational and transaction costs, as well as to gain vital credibility in the international financial market. The consolidated perspective, and the authority that goes with it, with clear accountability and sufficient scale, is needed to accumulate a competitive knowledge base and to be able to pay competitive but not market leading compensation. The scale of such a national champion enables it to be an attractive professional employer and gain the respect of all stakeholders.

The consolidated approach also facilitates a more complete understanding of the financial and fiscal risks of owning public assets, such as the intimate relationship often prevailing between state-owned commercial banks and state-owned enterprises, as in China, where state banks still seem to have a preference for extending credit to their state brethren. The banking system's inefficiency has a huge impact on China's economy. The country's banks incur higher costs than banks in Chile, Malaysia, Singapore, South Korea, or the US, where the average spread between loans and deposits is

3.1%. In China, after the money spent on capital injections into the banks has been included, the margin is 4.3%, which costs bank customers an extra US$25 billion a year, according to a study by McKinsey.[12] Even more expensive is the country's poor capital allocation, which sustains inefficient companies at the expense of more productive ones. Addressing this shortcoming would raise China's GDP by $259 billion, or 13%.

Both Abu Dhabi and China have started to address this issue by creating separate holding companies for their many state-owned banks. The Abu Dhabi Investment Council, established in 2007, is the holding company for the financial institutions owned by the government, reporting directly to the Executive Council, including National Bank of Abu Dhabi, Abu Dhabi Commercial Bank, Union National Bank, Al Hilal Bank, and Abu Dhabi National Insurance Company.

Central Huijin Investment is the Chinese government holding company responsible, together with the Ministry of Finance, for the "big four" state-owned commercial banks (some of the largest banks in the world) – Industrial and Commercial Bank of China, China Construction Bank, Bank of China, and Agricultural Bank of China – as well as China Development Bank, China Everbright Bank Co., and a number of other financial institutions.[13] Huijin was founded in 2003 as a subsidiary of SAFE within the central bank as the good banking vehicle after the restructuring and recapitalization of the banking sector. It was transferred from SAFE to become a wholly owned subsidiary of CIC, the Chinese SWF, in 2008.

Huijin has limited authority relative to the institutions it is assigned to monitor. It also competes with other stakeholders for the influence of the assets it is assigned to govern, and its governance structure is surrounded with ambiguity and a lack of responsibility and accountability. As an example, Huijin does not have the right to appoint, evaluate, or dismiss the chairmen of the financial institutions in its portfolio. The Organization Department of the CCP retains the privilege of appointing the executive chairmen and top managers of the holdings. It shares only a nominal responsibility for appointing board members together with the Ministry of Finance, with the CCP acting as the de facto owner, diluting accountability and authority of the nominal owners.

With the government being the ultimate provider of debt and equity, it requires a better understanding of the total fiscal and financial risk. This is another reason why the governments in China and Abu Dhabi are looking at further consolidating and professionalizing the ownership of their industrial assets.

In Abu Dhabi, the Executive Council, the executive authority of the Emirate of Abu Dhabi, has established the Office of State-owned Enterprises within the Executive Council. This is a first step to consolidate the previously fragmented management of its commercial assets, managed through three NWFs, Mubadala, Senaat, and International Petroleum Investment Company, as well as a number of other directly held assets, such as the airports, ports, nuclear energy, and other infrastructure assets, plus the stock exchange, airlines, and real estate. The National Oil Company (NOC), the country's main industrial asset, is still held directly by the Executive Council. As with other resource-rich countries at this stage of economic development, the NOC is likely to remain a separate part of the portfolio until the size of the oil and gas sector declines relative to the rest of the economy, that is, the country has successfully diversified from its dependence on oil and gas. The evolution of the oil and gas sector will have implications for continued state control and how the corporate governance model evolves. With improvement in NOC's corporate governance and transparency, it will be important to cope with growth in domestic and international operations.

The lessons from the financial crisis in hard-hit Dubai have also demonstrated the importance of the consolidation of commercial assets from a fiscal and financial risk perspective. With a fragmented approach, the government is missing not only the opportunity of a having a strategic portfolio approach to all the assets within its ownership, but also risks suboptimal capital allocation and potentially substantial financial and fiscal risk.

In China, SASAC (State-owned Assets Supervision and Administration Commission of the State Council), a special ministry directly under the State Council, was founded in 2003 and is responsible for managing some 117 large centrally owned companies, including some of the largest corporations in the world, such as Sinopec, State Grid, and China National Petroleum.[14] There are also regional and local SASACs at provincial and city levels holding local assets, such as corporates and real estate.

Because of the conflicting objectives of SASAC (a government legislator and controlling the ownership inside the government, but with the real control over these assets and their managers being with the CCP), it has proven less efficient in managing its corporate giants. With diminishing returns to the government but total compensation to the management rising, the current CCP leadership has failed to exercise any active management but is instead trying to regain control by launching an anti-corruption campaign combined with a drive to set a cap on executive pay. Well aware of the governance vacuum, the government wants to strengthen its governance and is looking at the experience of Temasek and its own CITIC.

CITIC (formerly China International Trust and Investment Corporation) is the Chinese state investment company, established in 1979 by Rong Yiren, one of the few pre-1949 industrialists who stayed behind and survived the communist revolution, on the initiative of Deng Xiaoping. CITIC was instrumental in opening up the Chinese economy to western investments. CITIC's original purpose was to attract and use foreign capital to modernize Chinese industry and business. In 2014, it made a reverse listing with its listed subsidiary in Hong Kong. The injection of $37 billion in group assets transformed not only the listed $6 billion Hong Kong offshoot into a $48 billion company but also the boundaries for how the state owns and manages commercial assets. Although representing only a small share of public wealth in China, it might once again show the way for a revolutionary transformation of the Chinese economy. Perhaps even western governments could learn something from CITIC, the brainchild of the Deng Xiaoping, and list their NWFs on the local stock markets. "It does not matter if the cat is black or white, as long as it catches the mouse," as Deng has been quoted saying.

The main argument for listing an NWF would be similar to that of obtaining a debt rating, it increases the number and broadens the spectrum of stakeholders interested in the development of the assets, along with a further strengthening of political independence, clear objectives and transparency. The counterarguments would be the fear of losing control and a source of clientelism. From an economic perspective, the marginal loss of control would be more than amply rewarded by the increase in yield and the economic growth generated by a more efficient performance of the assets in the portfolio. These financial and economic benefits might even compensate for the marginal loss of political influence.

chapter 11

Strategies for creating value

Most of this book is concerned with institutions that countries devise to govern public wealth. In this chapter, however, we will examine more closely how a national wealth fund might act vis-à-vis the public companies it governs in order to increase yield.

Clearly, better governance can make a big difference. Margaret Thatcher, hailed by many as the mother of privatization, started her then revolutionary path when elected in the face of a crumbling economy with significant portions of public assets in a morass of mismanagement. Her privatization revolution affected not only the western world but resounded globally, as she endeavored to sell off "the family silver" – to save the economy and the country from ruin. Nationalized industries in the UK at the time made up 10% of the British economy and consumed 14% of total capital investment. But rates of return on capital hovered somewhere between zero and 2%.[1]

Management in these industries was indifferent, customer service was nonexistent, and labor relations were extremely poor. Vested interests held the economy in a stranglehold, economically and culturally. These were obvious candidates for radical reform, and over the next two decades the wave of privatizations transformed public life, public finances, the stock market, and the consumer world, as everyone knew it.

These privatizations undoubtedly helped turn around the UK at the time, as also happened in many other developed economies. Critics have said that privatization merely transferred public wealth into private hands, and point to disastrous consequences in countries ruled by oligarchs. Others criticize poor deregulation of sectors where public firms were privatized. In reality, with a strong state, well-developed markets (commercial and capital), and a mature civil society, many developed economies have been able to transform large segments of their economies while still benefitting taxpayers, savers, investors, and, above all, consumers.

How poorly public wealth is governed is often only uncovered when a major financial crisis hits, as with Greece when the world learned more about how the Greek economy was one of the least open in Europe and thus one of the least competitive and most unequal, according to Pavlos Eleftheriadis. Greece had failed to address its deep structural problems because the country's own oligarchs had a vested interest in keeping things as they were.[2] This elite, a handful of families and their politicians, preserved their positions through the control of public assets, the media, and the banking system with old-fashioned favoritism.

A much cited example were the Greek railways, which spent 40% more on wages than they received in total revenues. Wages alone cost €246 million ($350 million), while revenues were €174 million ($250 million), and the total annual losses of €937 million ($1.4 billion) were five times income in 2009. This is certainly not the first example of a portfolio of value destroying government-owned businesses and crowding out private sector possibilities or initiatives, which ultimately contributed to bringing down the entire economy.

When western economies are again facing enormous challenges, governments might benefit from thinking more like an athlete and learning to make the best use of every muscle it has – improving yield from every asset. Once again, the UK seems to be at the forefront of a potential revolution by making an effort to map out how much property the central government and local governments own, as well as coming up with ideas on how to harvest these assets.

What is value creation?

Three different strategies converge to maximize the value of an asset/business; operational, business development, and capital structure strategies.

Operational strategy aims for the greatest possible efficiency in shaping the capabilities and methods of producing goods or services offered to the market to earn a profit. This means increasing productivity, although this often involves politically sensitive decisions such as making employees redundant, moving production and premises, or even shutting down and selling out completely in order to increase efficiency. With real estate, this would include looking at the usage per square foot, energy, and maintenance efficiency. Taking a more consolidated perspective on asset management would also allow for the centralized procurement of services and goods, which would have a substantial effect on the bottom line. Proper transparency enables benchmarking against the "best in class" in each sector. This is a good way to prevent vested interests from milking the assets and would maintain competitiveness in a business.

Business development focuses on increasing efficiency by shaping the organization to create value from customers, markets, and relationships. This part of value creation is less immediately apparent and would thereby seem less politically sensitive. However, done correctly, it aims to focus the organization on its core business and divest or close down operations that do not contribute to the core activity. With technological development as well as changes in the competitive environment, business models change and need to be constantly challenged. Well managed, this can generate substantial revenues. Badly managed, this could misuse owner funds (everyone's taxes) by fragmentation, or the opposite, creating a conglomerate of unrelated businesses.

Capital structure strategy reflects how a company finances its assets, overall operations, and growth. This is done using a combination of equity, debt, or hybrid securities. Capital structure strategy is the financing tool that helps operations and business development achieve the stated aims through optimal financing, thereby helping maximize yields and values from the business and assets. With real estate, this can have profound consequences on the value, as many public assets are simply forgotten, used by either clients of the government or a government entity that is not required to use that particular space in a prime city location. Government portfolios almost always contains stretches of land that are either not used at all and accounted for at zero value in the accounts, or where the original purpose has long since passed its usefulness for a government department. The most obvious place to look is often the military, where technological development can quickly make once vital installations completely irrelevant. Examples are numerous, from prime beachfront locations in New Zealand and entire islands in the Greek archipelago to the Annington housing estates in the UK.

Annington was formed in 1996 to acquire the Ministry of Defence's (MoD) Married Quarters Estate, consisting of some 57,000 residential properties. Annington is owned by the UK private equity fund Terra Firma, which leases back the majority of its properties to the MoD for accommodation for its married service personnel, with the MoD being responsible for the maintenance and upkeep of those properties. Properties that are released by the MoD are refurbished and available for sale or private rental at market prices. To date, only one-third of the portfolio assets have been sold in the open market.[3]

The balance between debt and equity funding needs to be aligned with the operating strategy and consider expected levels of capital spending and expected returns, liquidity and cash balances, risk management, and the expected (or required) dividend policy. Debt, as the cheaper source of funding, is often the largest component. But, too much debt (that is, overleveraging) can lead to default and insolvency, while too little debt may result in uncompetitive financial costs, thereby bringing a suboptimal value.

Historically, it was not unusual for governments to use public assets as off-balance sheet vehicles to raise additional funds for public spending, as with the Greek railway company. The Hellenic Railways Organisation had $13 billion in debt as of 2010, sales of less than $250 million, and more than $1 billion in annual losses. This debt alone represented approximately 5% of GDP out of a total US$33 billion in debt from all Greek SOEs. When this "off-balance sheet" debt was discovered by the so-called "troika" of international lenders (IMF, ECB, and the EU), it was immediately included in the country's official public debt.

The professional ownership and management of commercial assets requires, as we suggest, a ring-fenced institutional framework that enables operating at arm's length from government interference, as well as from a purely financial perspective. This enables better financial management and accounting, and facilitates lending at more efficient rates, using bond ratings and much more efficient risk management.

In the rest of this chapter, we will discuss the financial strategies available to portfolio owners – using debt, equity, or both, and how these can help improve the portfolio value.

The debt route

Using debt to finance a business venture or the acquisition of assets can have several advantages over equity financing. The cost of debt financing can be lower than that of equity financing because the interest paid to a debt investor (a bank or bondholder) is lower than the yield required from an equity investor.[4] Therefore, financing is preoccupied with pushing debt levels up as much as possible without tipping over the critical point where assets/operations risk losing their ability to pay the interest.

Debt financing allows managers to use a larger asset base. Using debt also introduces optionality for management, if this is properly consolidated in a professional institution, to perhaps develop an asset prior to sale and thereby avoid a fire sale.

Maximizing the value of public assets is not simply a financial matter. It is also important to the wider economy, and gives government an opportunity to show that it maintains a level playing field for all competitors including those in the private sector. Optimizing leverage facilitates the efficient use of public funds, which enables scarce equity capital to be used for other purposes – including returning it to the government as nominal owner, which should ultimately benefit taxpayers. Optimizing leverage prior to potential divestitures also limits the risk of selling the asset too cheaply.

Active governance requires a lot of the government as an owner. But selling or privatizing assets also requires a lot from a government in terms of acting as a professional seller.

The use of debt financing requires government to manage public assets as a consolidated portfolio, and also requires government to install professional management of the asset portfolio for several reasons, not least to avoid taking excessive risks and overleveraging. Many government officials have found themselves overwhelmed by the challenge of overleveraged public assets due to their lack of insight, transparency, and coordination between asset administrators, that is, the general lack of professional management.

State assets subject to crony capitalism are regularly prevented from being managed efficiently or privatized, due to their large debts to industrial or banking interests connected with a local oligarch. This is common in the cases of many failed privatizations in economies in the former Soviet states and southern Europe.

Further, many resource-rich countries with an abundance of capital end up pouring enormous amounts of equity into the firms they buy, and then end up with large amounts of debt that these firms accumulate. This often happens where rulers or governments lack a consolidated portfolio strategy, understanding of capital allocation, and proper transparency of financial returns. In addition to overleveraging or the continual need for capital injections, it is also common that off-balance sheet financing is used – ostensibly to preserve the assets in public ownership, but this only further increases financial and fiscal risk.

With a consolidated portfolio and professional management, the key benefit derived from pre-privatization financing lies in the ability to increase the value of a monetized asset in a way that produces net benefits. This also allows flexibility in the timing of the sale by removing potential budgetary pressures that might force premature disposal, instead of waiting to realize maximum value, that is, the timing can be chosen to ensure the asset is not simply sold at a fire sale.

As an example, local governments in the UK have developed a model for local regeneration called the local asset backed vehicle (LABV), a joint venture into which the council assigns key property and land that the private sector is able to borrow against. Risk and reward are shared through a limited liability partnership and can help avoid the lengthy procurement periods and startup costs of previous public–private partnerships. Project finance is usually provided for town center development, such as the £450 million, 25-year partnership between Croydon Borough Council and the developer John Laing. LABVs offer a chance to leverage council assets without having to dispose of them.[5] The government of Greece considered a similar structure, after facing difficulties in privatizing its assets.

In this structure, assets should be transferred to a professionally managed corporate entity owned by the government able to raise pre-privatization financing either against future cash flows or the intrinsic value of each underlying asset. At maturity of such a deal, the entity could sell the assets on the market to repay the financing, or it can transfer the asset to the financing institution as repayment. In the Greek example, the state could thereby gain time to implement necessary structural reforms, which would enhance the asset's value.

The government would retain control over the asset and, most importantly, can still freely sell the asset when and if it can get fair value. This would generate much needed private sector liquidity for the nation, which could be used to repay current debt or develop other assets in their portfolio. At the same time, the government would also retain a partial upside in the recovery of asset valuations over time, while having irrevocably started the privatization process.

An NWF created using this model would also be able to issue securities in its own name based on its own credit rating as a separate corporate entity. It may first have to establish a track record and build its credibility as an owner, developer, and operator of assets, such as Temasek, Kazahnah, Mubadala, and SIG.

Since property is the least transparent, but often the largest asset class in most government portfolios, this would require special attention early in any monetization process. Separately ring-fencing a property portfolio and creating a coherent, viable, structured property development strategy would enable a variety of value creation alternatives. Financing could then be tailored to the cash-generating nature of the properties, that is, their rent-producing properties, sale and lease back, properties needing development/restructuring, and special use properties, or others lacking commercial value.

Applying a value creation perspective to properties where the government is both owner and tenant has the additional benefit of setting a market price on the rental cost of these premises. This creates incentives for the state to relocate out of unnecessarily expensive rental properties. The efficiency effect this produces can significantly reduce state expenditures. Incentives would be aligned to increase the value of the property as well as decrease government costs, by optimizing the efficient use of floor space and increasing the number of private sector tenants renting from the property portfolio.

The equity route

The equity route can involve the entire spectrum of transactions from selling just a few shares in a core business, or all the shares in a subsidiary or a demerged portion of a commercial business. This can be through an IPO or a standard trade sale. An IPO can help broaden the stakeholder base and thereby increase pressure for reform, through greater transparency, better governance, and professional management. A trade sale can improve competitive advantage through operational, financial, and strategic benefits usually found with an industrial buyer, by leveraging the attention, focus, and managerial skills offered by a financial buyer.

In many cities worldwide, there are vast spaces of land waiting to be developed, such as Hellenikon, the old airport in Athens right on the beach of what is known as the Greek Riviera. In Istanbul, military security zones occupy more than 50,000 acres, most of it green space and much of it in prized locations beside the waterways of the Bosphorus and the Golden Horn, including the old Greek commercial district of Galata. This is the site of a $700 million project to build a new port complex, while a vast, deserted shipyard on the Golden Horn, occupied by the army, will be turned into a complex including two marinas, two five-star hotels, a shopping mall, and a mosque with space for 1,000 worshippers, in a project tendered for $1.3 billion. The government has given a 60-year lease to Dogus, the Turkish family-owned conglomerate representing the winning consortium, to develop the port and the real estate. This is a recent example where a government brings in private sector capital and expertise to develop its assets more commercially.

From a tactical point of view, the privatization of business operations can be seen from two perspectives: one is the sale of a business already operating in a competitive market, and the other the sale of a former monopoly.

The main concern of a government selling a competitive business is that of a "seller." The government can then focus on representing the existing shareholders, otherwise known as taxpayers. The government's fiduciary duty should make the primary objective the maximization of value and thus sell at the highest price possible, as would any private investor. Whether an IPO or a trade sale will bring the best price depends on current market circumstances and on how well developed the assets are.

A recent example is the privatization of Royal Mail in the UK at the end of 2013. This former utility now works in a rather well-developed and competitive market. The UK government was heavily criticized for the pricing of the shares and was said to have achieved even poorer value for money for taxpayers than the state sell-offs of the 1980s and 90s. The government sold 60% of the company, raising nearly £2 billion ($3.4 billion). But the shares rose 38% on the first day of trading, attracting claims that taxpayers had lost as much as £1 billion ($1.7 billion). This can be compared to the IPOs in the 1980s and 90s where the first day rise in the share price ranged from 14% in British Aerospace to 86% for British Telecom.[6]

Perhaps this is simply the price politicians must pay to weaken resistance from vested interests against the sale, inviting large numbers of employees to buy shares cheaply alongside institutional buyers. In comparison, in Sweden, the IPO of Telia was priced at the highest it could possibly achieve at that point in time. This brought criticism from the large number of retail investors that had bought into the sale for not being an immediately beneficial investment.

With regard to the sale of a former monopoly, the government's tactical considerations are not only that of taxpayers getting a maximum sales price, but also the long-term consumer perspective. In order to privatize a utility properly, the government must also consider the regulatory framework and supervisory institution. This demands creating transparency in service levels as well as pricing, and establishing a level playing field for new entrants followed by firm regulation to ensure fair play.

In this context, failure to construct an effective market mechanism raises the risk of creating private sector oligopolies and hidden state subsidies instead. The need for price intervention illustrates the risks of privatizing state-owned utilities.

In reality, most privatizations are somewhere in between these two perspectives. The important issue for the government, however, is always to get the sequencing right. Paving the way for privatization with proper regulation is critical. If the regulatory balance is wrong or the competitive structure ineffective, the consumer ends up paying too much, corporate profits become "too" high, and private sector shareholders receive a "free ride" from taxpayers – as critics often expound.[7] But regulation is not a final destination, it is a complex process under considerable uncertainty.

In the end, it is more likely that the consumer will benefit from an individual private business slugging it out with a strong government regulator, rather than a Leviathan government owner fighting with itself over regulatory issues. Nationalized assets are shielded from competition, financial pressure, and often from regulatory requirements compared to private sector operations. Under national control, these assets tend to become conglomerates or even business empires. Selling noncore assets will generate substantial funds, and simultaneously improve focus on the original core business, which should increase the asset's value.

Separating or demerging operations with no apparent relevance to each other, or transferring noncore assets and services into a dedicated asset management company, can be an expedient way of making the core business immediately free to specialize and achieve the necessary focus and thereby rapidly increase operational efficiency and asset value. In private business, these strategies are considered continuously by owners and managers everywhere to maintain or improve efficiency and stay ahead of the competition.

European governments have spent the past three decades breaking up and privatizing their integrated general postal operations into the three obvious constituent parts: telephone networks, the postal system, and a post office network. This started in 1981 with Margaret Thatcher's plans to privatize British Telecom, which went through in 1984. But she balked at privatizing Royal Mail, saying she was "not prepared to have the Queen's head privatized." After more than 30 years, Royal Mail is now privatized, but this did not include the network of post office branches, which the government plans to convert to a mutual institution after pouring over £3 billion ($4.7 billion) into its 11,500 outdated branch offices.

Meanwhile, in the Netherlands, KPN was floated in 1994 and subsequently split into two companies, one for telecommunications and one for mail, express delivery, and logistics (renamed TNT Post Group), which then divested the post office network separately. In Germany, Deutsche Post was listed in 2000 and has since had profit margins double that of the Royal Mail. International competitors have also established operations in the UK, including FedEx, the US operator, and DHL (owned by Deutsche Post), benefitting both consumers and businesses. Separately, Sweden and other countries generated considerable value by further streamlining their operations for telecoms, mail, and post offices.

The remarkable story of the world's largest postal service

Between 1947 and 1995, Deutsche Bundespost was a monopoly responsible for postal services and telecommunications. In 1995, its three services were transformed into three stock corporations: Deutsche Post, Deutsche Telekom, and Deutsche Postbank. Today, Deutsche Post is the largest postal company in the world. How did this happen?

Initially, the state held all shares but private shareholders were accepted. The state kept the majority of shares for five years.

In the following years, the efficiency and service of the post increased due to investments. Since 1998, 90% of letters are automatically sorted (compared to 25% in the beginning of the 1990s). After a restructuring of inland services and organization, Deutsche Post invested in services and acquisitions abroad. In 1998, it acquired 10% of the shares in DHL, and together with DHL, established the Euro Express for letters and parcels in 20 European countries. It also bought Global Mail (US), the largest private international letter service provider in the US.

In 1999, Deutsche Post acquired the Swiss logistic company Danzas as well as Air Express International, the biggest US service provider for international air cargo. Moreover, Deutsche Post bought the shares of the Deutsche Postbank from the German state. At the end of 2000, Deutsche Post went public and was listed on the stock exchange. In 2002, the shareholding in DHL was increased to 100% and Deutsche Post also acquired a 25% share of Lufthansa Cargo, which belonged to DHL. In 2004, Deutsche Postbank went public. In 2005, Deutsche Post acquired Exel, the British logistic enterprise. Moreover, after the Reconstruction Loan Cooperation sold its share of Deutsche Post, the majority of Deutsche Post shares were no longer held by the state.

In 2008, Deutsche Post launched its GoGreen climate protection program and opened its new air cargo hub in Leipzig/Halle Airport. In 2009, now called Deutsche Post DHL, it started selling Postbank to Deutsche Bank, which was completed in 2012. In 2012, the DHL Express North Asia Hub was extended at Shanghai Pudong International Airport. Further investments were made in 2013. In Germany, Deutsche Post started to establish intercity transport. In the US, at Cincinnati/Northern Kentucky International Airport, the air cargo hub for the American continent was extended.

Today, Deutsche Post acts in 220 countries and employs 480,000 people and is comfortably profitable. Business volumes in 2013 amounted to €55 billion (US$71 billion). This can be seen as a success of sorts, but it is also gamble using German taxpayers as venture capitalists.

When countries consolidate their public holdings into a portfolio, it is often a first step in improving transparency. Governments often end up realizing they control thousands of smaller assets, with China being the extreme example – in the mid-1990s it found that it owned more than 120,000 "enterprises." Consolidation takes on a different meaning in such situations. The Chinese called it "grasping the large and letting go of the small."[8] The idea was to concentrate on the larger assets where government ownership was considered relevant at that stage of the asset's development, while letting go of everything else. This often first involved an effort to incorporate the activity altogether, to attach only the physical assets that reasonably belong to the production/service, thus creating a legal entity that can be sold, while discontinuing activities that are dormant or no longer viable. Efforts to sell off smaller state-owned operations – often to managers and employees – often provide a cornerstone for private sector development in the country.

In its policy of "grasping the large and letting go the small," China undertook the largest restructuring effort of this kind by any government. It was adopted in 1997 and laid the foundation for central government efforts to consolidate and manage its public assets.[9] The mass privatizations of smaller businesses to managers and employees consolidated the central government portfolio to some 37,000 smaller entities and 169 larger enterprises by 2004.[10]

The conditions for value creation

The first step toward enabling improving portfolio value for any government is consolidating the ownership and management of the entire public assets portfolio – bringing together all the assets under a single management – everything from corporates, infrastructure, and financial institutions, along with property asset portfolios.

Some tribal-oriented cultures or weak state economies often have a strong tendency to follow a "divide and conquer" mentality, which requires any portfolio to be divided up between several holding companies instead of establishing a single interface toward the markets. The arguments for consolidating under a single management are considerable, both from the perspective of the markets and an organizational point of view.

The market perspective argues for a focused approach toward potential investors, be it debt or equity. This ensures a coherent and timely presentation of assets designed to achieve the most attractive pricing. Such focus allows a segmented presentation with identifiable risk profiles, and enables merging with related assets (public or private) to create an even more attractive investment profile when appropriate. Moreover, this will contribute to lower operational and transactional costs.

From an operational perspective, a single holding company establishes clear accountability with a consolidated hierarchy and transparent lines of authority. Consolidation will also create sufficient critical mass to enable accumulating a competitive knowledge base and paying competitive (although not necessarily market leading) compensation, so as to become an attractive employer.

chapter 12

Lessons for future national wealth funds

Previous chapters have described various countries' attempts to reform governance of public assets or even implement national wealth funds. In this chapter, we summarize the lessons one can draw from these attempts, and the way forward.

An incorporated holding company, a national wealth fund (NWF), is a professional steward of public assets, which can then be charged with developing and managing those assets and realizing their best value through potential sales that maximize long-term economic value consistent with the principles of rationality, public interest, and transparency. The holding company would also be a better vehicle to improve access to debt financing and potentially reduce the cost of borrowing on international capital markets – for financing infrastructure projects or other commercial ventures.

The professional independence of an NWF is helped by clear objectives and ensuring it acts openly and transparently. This professional independence works two ways, being particularly important to the political establishment in connection with any restructuring prior to privatization of a specific holding. The NWF management crucially needs professional independence to gain credibility in international capital markets, much like many central banks have done after becoming "independent" of short-term government meddling. These arguments were first highlighted by Walter Bagehot, who argued for independent central banking in the 19th century with his book *Lombard Street*, but it took nearly 100 years for these ideas to gain acceptance.[1] NWFs should be organized along the following lines.

Corporate governance

To solidify its independence, the NWF should operate under a corporate governance structure based on the highest international standards, where the directors and managers would be entirely responsible for and held accountable in ensuring the optimization of performance, value creation, and the yield of the portfolio.

Establishing and publishing a clear chain of command that clearly identifies accountability at every level is a vital first step. This could be stated in a transparent ownership policy issued by the government with a set of rules of procedure for the board of directors, which would then be published and applied by the NWF for all its holdings, specifically to avoid overlap of responsibility or the possibility of undue political interference.

Since we are talking about commercial assets, there is no reason why publicly owned assets should not be subject to the same legal framework and requirements as private sector owners and their directors. In many countries, the functions and responsibilities of boards are clearly defined by law, with government-owned companies having the same responsibility and accountability as boards in joint stock companies.

Establishing a level playing field for private and publicly owned companies ensures that both are subject to a single legal framework and public assets are able to use all the tools of the private sector. In addition, some countries, like New Zealand, issue a formal ownership policy, which is a central declaration of accountability for all involved. In these, the government clearly delineates the board's role in broad strategic terms, which includes the preparation, finalization, and implementation of a statement of corporate intent.[2]

The board's effectiveness and political independence depend on the strength, quality, and structure of the institutional environment. All the components and roles, such as "board" and "director," vary between different jurisdictions, which is why any solution needs to be tailored to the individual situation in each country. The division of responsibilities for effective boards varies depending on jurisdiction as well as local regulations. However, three primary governance functions remain relatively universal. These are:

1 *Supervision:* mainly risk management and auditing
2 *Decision making:* strategy and compensation as well as human resources
3 *Execution:* day-to-day management and accounting.

These functions are assigned differently, ranging from the market-based unitary Anglo-Saxon system to the greater, control-based "two-tier" system in the continental or Germanic system, with the Nordic model combining characteristics of both.[3]

To improve governance and strengthen political independence, proper delegation of responsibility combined with some form of checks and balances is generally preferable. This could include supervision that is somehow covered and separated from the executive function, such as separating the role of the chairman from that of the CEO. A professional nonexecutive chairman, with the appropriate commercial knowledge and experience to match company management while maintaining the trust of the entity's political masters, adds informal credibility to the political independence toward all stakeholders.

In contrast, the absence of a meaningful institutional framework can make the entire board structure more or less irrelevant. In an economy with a weak central government, the ability to appoint friends and family to the boards of SOEs is sometime reminiscent of the days of royal bequests of land used to create allegiances and an additional source of income for an ally. Such feudal-like behavior would be hard to address as an isolated issue, but should be seen in the wider context of reforms to strengthen central government. In countries with a strong central government, on the other hand, dominated by a single political party, the nomination function becomes a tool to extend party influence. As an example, the Organization Department of the Central Committee of the CCP retains the privilege of appointing the executive chairmen and top managers of state companies and banks, with the chairman and the party secretary often being one and the same, reporting directly to the party rather than the nominal owner (the government ministry, or holding company), while the supervisory board reports directly to the State Council.[4] These boards are therefore weak and the combined power of chairman, CEO and party head makes any ownership management vehicle, including a holding company, largely irrelevant.

With the introduction of an ownership policy, as was done in Sweden, governments can clearly define the limits of involvement, such as setting the company vision, appointing external auditors, and nominating nonexecutive directors. The board, through its chair, should coordinate its views with representatives of the owner(s) on issues of critical importance and, if necessary, propose a resolution at the shareholders' meeting. Foremost among such issues are major strategic changes in the company operations (acquisitions, mergers, or divestments) and decisions that entail substantial changes in the company risk profile or balance sheet.[5]

The contractual relationship between the owner (the government) and the NWF should be limited to the government or parliament appointing board members and auditors for the NWF, and establishing its overall purpose and strategy, as well as agreeing on a dividend policy.

The NWF should be self-reliant in managing risk, although with proper internal controls and internal competence rather than relying on, or even seen to be relying on, the government to be the ultimate guarantor of risk. Furthermore, specialized committees such as remuneration and auditing would be required within a supervisory board, to further demonstrate their ability to remain independent of the owner. The independent selection of external auditors should remain a function of the owners or, when applicable, the supervisory board. Internal audit and controls and then perhaps especially risk management would be a cornerstone in supporting political independence within the NWF.

Perhaps the successful development of independent central banks could provide guidance. Questions raised (even by Walter Bagehot) regarding such independence are familiar to this day, including:

- preserving accountability while insulating central bankers from political interference
- ensuring central bankers devote their attention to their duties
- calculating the optimal size for decision-making committees
- obtaining financial sector representation in central bank decision making while preventing capture of the central bank by the financial sector.

The measurement of central bank independence generally focuses on four aspects:

1 management is insulated from political pressure by means of tenure security and independent appointment
2 freedom from government interference in policy decisions
3 clearly defined monetary policy objectives
4 restrictions that limit lending to the government.[6]

Along with transparency, the above are necessary conditions for the proper management of public assets and would also help support the credibility and independence of even an NWF.

Appointing and evaluating the board

In order to support, as well as to be seen to support, a transfer of the supervisory responsibility to the board of the NWF, there needs to be a professional and institutional nomination process to populate the board that can win the trust of all stakeholders. This would ensure that the ultimate selection criteria are justifiable as based on relevant competence. The optimal combination of competence will change over time. A proper board nomination process must therefore not only be based on a board evaluation but also be rooted in the current business plan and adjust the competence/skill mix required at that point in time.

A similar professional delegation of responsibility and accountability should then be placed on the board of each holding, including the professional and institutional nomination process managed by the NWF to populate the boards of each holding according to merit.

Trust in the governance structure of the NWF rests in no small part on the independence and credibility of the supervisory function of a board, regardless of the legislative model. It is crucial for a functioning governance structure that this board is clearly established as the main body responsible for the portfolio. Unless this responsibility is fully vested and clearly understood and communicated, the government will not be able to transfer its responsibility for the assets, but will remain the culprit for success or failure.

As an example, the Riksbank, the Swedish central bank, has a General Council of eleven members, appointed by the Swedish parliament, with a chairman and a vice-chairman appointed by the members among themselves. The day-to-day activities of the Riksbank are managed by an executive board, consisting of six members, who are appointed by the General Council for a period of five or six years. The General Council appoints the chairman of the executive board, who at the same time shall be the governor of the Riksbank, and at least one vice-chairman, who will also serve as deputy governor of the Riksbank.[7] A member of the General Council may not, according to the law, be a Cabinet minister, a member of the Riksbank's executive board, a member or deputy of a board of directors of a bank or any other company subject to supervision by the Financial Supervisory Authority, or hold any other employment or assignment which makes him unsuitable as a member of the General Council.

In dynastic-like societies (based on family, religion, or party affiliation), state companies are sometimes seen as if part of national and "dynastic" security, where higher posts could only be trusted to be held within "the family" or party. Another perspective would be to act like successful family dynasties such as the Ottomans, the longest ruling family dynasty in history, outsourcing the most vital parts of governments such as defense and government administration to an independent professional elite – the devşirme system (the notorious "blood tax"). The intention of the system was to maintain an equilibrium in society while still ensuring the most professional development. This was done through an elite of non-Turkish administrators and soldiers as a balance of power between the ruling dynasty and other aristocratic families. Thus, even for a dynastic-like owner or autocratic ruler it makes sense to hire external professionals to manage its assets. This would not only prevent compromising the professional relationship between owner and manager, facilitating replacement of underperforming managers, but it would also prevent any side within a "dynasty" or clan to gain relative power through the affiliation with powerful commercial operations. Although the concept of hiring professionals to run the "family" business has merits even in today's world, we would recommend a more modern way of recruiting and incentivizing international professionals than the methods used by the Ottomans' devşirme system.

In more critical financial situations, board nominations could be used as the tool to change the course of a company. In the restructuring of the Swedish portfolio in the late 1990s, professionals were appointed to more than four-fifths of all board positions almost within the first year of the three-year reform project.

Losing the ability to influence board appointments is perhaps the single biggest reason why politicians, even in developed economies otherwise seen as champions of meritocracy, resist moving the ownership unit from inside government to an independent holding company, as that would take away from politicians the power to appoint all the board members to the NWF.

Professional management

Attracting the right talent to run state-owned assets as well as the NWF requires the relevant policies and corporate governance structure. This should certainly include pay and incentive structures, but is equally a matter of freedom from political interference and overblown public criticism. In the UK, this is proving a major problem. The body overseeing the banks in public ownership, a government entity, is struggling to find nonexecutives and a chairman. Likewise, the banks themselves are finding that government ownership brings extra scrutiny of compensation, which in the US and the UK may prove a big competitive handicap on those banks that cannot quickly repay Troubled Asset Relief Program funds or exit UK government ownership.

To succeed, the executive management of an NWF should be similar to that of a private equity fund, with relevant management and sector experience from international finance, industry, or private equity.

The initial management team would not have to be very extensive, but a limited group of professionals of around 20 employees, supported by a cadre of external professionals and auditors assisting management on a project-by-project basis. The team would grow, over time, to 35–40 professionals.

The senior management team would consist of a small number of professionals including the CEO, ultimately responsible for the execution of the strategy, together with a chief operating officer, responsible for compliance and risk management and a head of legal affairs. The CFO would have a treasurer and a debt structuring specialist within their responsibility, as well as professionals with responsibility for investor relations, communications, and the capability and ownership of its IT systems in order to have control of accounting and cash management.

As is common in private equity, the management of the portfolio would benefit from being divided into relevant sectors teams, such as TMT, energy, financial institutions, general industry, real estate, and so on. Each sector team would be headed by an investment executive with extensive international experience as an industrial executive, sector head of international investment banks, or private equity firms. One or two investment managers would support each sector team. They should have a background in financial and industrial analysis, project management skills for each relevant equity and debt transaction, as well as restructurings where relevant. Senior management and the sector teams would also be supported by a network of industrial advisers, consisting of experienced senior executives from the relevant industries. This network of industrial advisers would help form the nonexecutive boards of each holding, as well as participating as independent advisers on other specific holdings where relevant.

The NWF will provide expertise and help each asset to grow and develop through the implementation of industrial strategies geared toward growth and operational excellence. The strategies laid out for each portfolio company are executed by the CEO of the holding, with the support of the board led by an independent chairman. The chairman and the nonexecutive directors would be independent business executives. For wholly owned portfolio companies, it would be sufficient with one representative from the NWF, while for listed holdings, the NWF could potentially nominate an industrial adviser from the network of advisers as a nonexecutive director.

The chairman of each holding is the main point of contact between the NWF and the CEO of the holding, as well as between the board and the NWF. For wholly owned companies, the dedicated industrial adviser and the investment executive would create an informal sounding board for the chairman in his support the CEO of the portfolio company. This is vital when transforming a former monopoly into a competitive business, or any other major strategic reorientation or shift in the business.

The transparency and continuous performance evaluation of the CEO, chairman and board of directors, as well as the investment advisory professional, is assessed once a year in a comprehensive process and set against the business plan and market analysis. This process ensures that relevant competences are present on the board and that governance works in accordance with objectives and relevant market outlook. This evaluation can lead to changes in the board composition.

The additional concern of an NWF, compared to what preoccupies the standard private equity setup, is the constant need to be vigilant as regards short-term political influence and other vested interests. This is a continuous threat to the value maximization objective and requires the awareness of the board and executive management, as well as the support of other financial stakeholders. Meanwhile, the cultural, financial, and operational challenges to transforming a former monopoly into a fully functioning market-oriented business would be the same for a private owner as for a government.

Political independence is ultimately about the trust and confidence given to the institution and its representative. Trust is a measure of belief in the honesty or good intentions of another party, while confidence is our belief in the competence of the trusted. Trust reduces social complexity and allows for more efficient interactions that might otherwise be too complex to be considered or much more time-consuming, specifically for cooperation,[8] as in the everyday world of road traffic management or business. For example, at a traffic intersection, we trust other drivers to act in a prescribed fashion so as to enable the traffic to change course smoothly and efficiently, while in business, trust that a certain business transaction will take place in the future is shown with a handshake or a written contract. Generally, a failure in trust may be forgiven more easily if it is interpreted as a failure of competence rather than a lack of benevolence or honesty.

There are two components to political independence: the institutional and the personal. Both are aiming to create trust in the intentions of the government to allow for the NWF to be professional, independent, and free from short-term political influence. The institutional component involves the legal structure and framework in and around the holding company, its system of governance, and articles of associations. The personal component involves the human factors influencing our ability to trust the idea of political independence and the people set to act as agents, including the selection process to nominate the board.

In economics, trust is often conceptualized as reliability in transactions and has a circular relationship, such as perceived justice leads to trust that, in turn, promotes future perceptions of justice.[9] Trust will also increase with the open exchange of information, which is why transparency is a crucial component for political independence.[10]

Trust is an evolving process that requires persistence and openness about the intentions and competence of the institutional system and the persons that represent it. Trust requires complete transparency. Transparency should be understood as the capability of the public and investors to understand the nature and status of all assets held and managed within the NWF. The quality and reliability of information has to be held in the highest regard to ensure the viability of any marketable initiative, which includes retaining independent auditing and valuation of the assets. An NWF should maintain transparency with respect to its portfolio of assets to the same extent as any publicly listed vehicle, issuing regular public market communications, including annual reports and quarterly portfolio reviews. A good example from the private sector is Investor AB, the listed Swedish asset management company controlled by the Wallenberg family. On the public sector side, Solidium, the Finnish government holding company, provides similar good transparency, although it is not listed.

Boards in state-owned commercial enterprises should be held responsible for compliance with generally accepted accounting and reporting standards, in addition to current accounting legislation and generally accepted accounting principles. Larger holdings or those with strategic importance should also follow the international practice of listed companies. These large state assets should be required to publish their annual reports and financial statements in English and audited by reputable auditors. The ownership vehicle should also have a dedicated English website, publishing its annual reports and audited financial statements, also with quarterly financial data based on best international practice.

Real estate in an NWF

The real estate segment of public commercial assets is seldom fully included in the consolidated management of an NWF. This has a price for two reasons. First, financially, because the diversity and scale would improve the access or cost of borrowing on the international capital markets for the financing of infrastructure projects or other commercial ventures or assets. Second, economically, because an integrated business plan across asset classes would not only give flexibility to maximize value and act on any potential divestiture at the individually most advantageous timing, but also because economies of scale would be able to lower transaction and operational costs.

However, a number of governments have created specialized holding companies for some of their real estate assets, including Finland, Austria, the UK, and Sweden, demonstrating an ability to produce a healthy rate of return. The holding companies come in two main models, fragmented and consolidated. The fragmented model, represented by Sweden, is where the original owners, often a government ministry, vested their real estate assets into a holding company. The consolidated version, represented by Finland, is where the central government has attempted to consolidate several different real estate segments from a wide range of original owners within the government under a single holding company.

The main benefit with the fragmented approach, for example that taken by Sweden in the 1990s, is political. With the original owner, such as a government department/ministry, setting up its own holding company, the financial benefits are, at least temporarily, maintained with the original owner. Tactically, this avoids or delays the internal battle of ownership inside the government, until a later date. While improving transparency is improved considerably and irrevocably, this solution benefits from many of the operational benefits of vesting the assets into a private sector vehicle.

Publicly owned real estate is often found in four different categories:

1 *Administrative buildings:* including the real estate housing central government ministries and authorities.
2 *Departmental assets:* including assets belonging to the ministry of defense, which is often one of the largest owners of real estate in a

country, including naval bases, airfields, living accommodation for military personnel, scientific facilities, storage and distribution centers, communications facilities, and offices; the ministry of transport with assets such as ports and airports; the ministry of health with hospitals; and the ministry of education with schools and universities.

3 *SOEs:* real estate assets belonging to former monopolies such as the railways, post, telecoms, and electricity networks.

4 *Other:* central government is often the largest owner of forestry assets in a country and could also hold vast tracts of agricultural land or simply undeveloped land that could have unrealized social and financial value if properly managed. Some countries may also have urban properties such as the Crown Estate in the UK or Vasakronan in Sweden.

No country has consolidated assets from all four categories into one single holding company, although Finland has probably come the furthest with its Senate Properties under the ministry of education. Sweden went down the decentralized route and put all real estate assets connected with a number of ministries and SOEs into different holding companies, such as:

- Akademiska Hus: higher education assets
- Vassallen: former barracks owned by the ministry of defence
- Sveaskog: forestry assets
- Jernhusen: real estate assets of the state railway company
- National Property Board of Sweden (Statens Fastighetsverk): core administrative real estate assets. This public service entity manages some 2,300 properties and 6.4 million hectares of land, representing one-seventh of the surface area of Sweden. It includes all Swedish embassies, ministerial buildings, country residences and institutions, and 7 of the 14 Swedish world heritage sites on UNESCO's list. With bodies such as the Swedish National Heritage Board, the Swedish Fortifications Agency, and the Swedish Maritime Authority, it shares responsibility for the country's 300 or so state-owned historic buildings.

The main purpose of using a private sector framework is to leverage the existing accounting methodologies and corporate structures to improve transparency through a complete register of the assets and a potential market value in order to understand or at least enable an assessment of the potential alternative use of each property.

The UK has surprisingly initiated a number of uncoordinated initiatives to improve transparency of its pubic commercial assets. Yet it is difficult to reach satisfactory results using different accounting methods and no national approach to a country-wide register or cadaster. Furthermore, central government has maintained its fragmented approach to ownership, whereby each department has maintained ownership of commercial assets and only institutionalized a centralized advisory function. However, even this advisory function is fragmented, divided into two separate government bodies and staffed by civil servants and the third unit set up as a Companies Act company:

1 The Shareholder Executive: oversees a range of corporate and corporate-like assets, as a part of the Department for Business, Innovation & Skills.
2 The Government Property Unit: oversees some of the government's real estate assets, and is a part of the Cabinet Office.
3 UK Financial Investments, a limited company wholly owned by HM Treasury, manages the government's investments in RBS, Lloyds, and UK Asset Resolution Ltd.

In addition, the Crown Estate, a limited company, is one of the largest property owners in the UK, with a portfolio worth around £8 billion, including a large number of properties in central London, the Windsor Estate, shopping centers, 144,000 hectares of agricultural land and forests, more than half the UK's foreshore, wind farms, and so on.

A private sector company would normally consolidate its holdings into a centralized vehicle to optimize the use of space and minimize operational costs, including energy, waste and water, as well as maintenance and cleaning. For the same reasons, the government, seen as an enterprise, would benefit from consolidating its commercial real estate under a centralized holding company in order to avoid financial inefficiency through incoherency and lack of transparency, or suboptimal management. Developing real estate, including selling and acquiring assets and contracting developers, benefits greatly from professional management and a private sector structure able to incentivize the appropriate management in order to maximize value for the government and society as a whole.

13

We all want to build roads now, but can we afford it?

Railways and commercial airlines were, in their early days, seen as vital parts of a country's transport infrastructure, like roads and bridges. The government often owned and maintained the infrastructure of a public service, or quickly nationalized it. In addition, governments also set the fares and routes and protected their assets by restricting new entrants. These state champions were also vital parts of the national war machine, sending troops to the front. After World War II, these state champions, along with the network of post offices, were seen as integral building blocks in the construction of the welfare state.

For several decades now, most countries have underinvested in sorely needed public infrastructure such as roads, railroads, and other public transport, as well as water, wastewater, and electricity networks. Especially in developed economies, this has happened because the political process often gives priority to short-term expenditure rather than long-term investments. At the same time, countries also often invest in bridges to nowhere and spectacular projects without paying heed to what renders the highest social return. The IMF (2014) concluded that investments in public infrastructure have fallen over time and that more investment could actually stimulate growth. But it also points out that the efficiency of infrastructure investment can be much improved in most countries.

Roads, railroads, and other public infrastructure are often state assets that are not treated as assets because they do not render financial returns, and cannot easily be sold or transferred. They generate no revenue. And, in fact, they are not included in the estimates of the value of public assets that we presented in earlier chapters.[1] Still, they can often be put to much better use without compromising their primary function.

In this chapter, we will explore these issues and show how independent holding companies can be an excellent tool for diverting public wealth toward infrastructure and giving these a sounder economic footing.

Boom and bust in infrastructure

China has produced a large number of world infrastructure records, such as the largest hydroelectric project – the Three Gorges Dam – and 4,000 miles of high-speed rail. It has also scattered new airports and railway terminals across the land. This infrastructure boom will continue for some time yet. Over the next 20 years, the BRIC countries (Brazil, Russia, India, and China) will account for more than 50% of the growth in road travel and more than 40% of the growth in air travel.

In spite of such spectacular infrastructure projects, the more common sight in BRIC countries as well as rich countries is a lack of infrastructure and maintenance. For example, the Kiel Canal in the German state of Schleswig-Holstein – the world's busiest man-made waterway, which connects the North Sea and the Baltic Sea – had to be partially closed last year after two wornout locks, built in 1914, broke down. The famous German autobahns are crowded, causing commuters to waste eight working days per year in traffic jams. Major bridges crossing the River Rhine are so dilapidated that they have been off-limits for heavy lorries, while ordinary cars must slow down to a demeaning 38 mph. Germany, which can easily afford more, is one of the many countries that has been neglecting to maintain its roads, railways, and waterways, resulting in a huge investment backlog (although it has spent much more modernizing the former communist East). Public investment plummeted from 13% of federal spending in 1998 to less than 10% today. Government investment currently constitutes only 15.4% of total investment in Germany, which puts the country in 25th place among 31 industrial countries.

In many other countries, the situation is even worse. Yet, infrastructure can conceivably work much better with improved management. Here are some examples.

Better infrastructure management can achieve wonders

In some places, infrastructure investments turn out to be profitable and extremely well run without much government planning. Compare Tokyo's private railroads with the US government-owned system.

Tokyo is one of the world's largest megacities, with a population of 35 million. Instead of the expected traffic chaos, vast numbers of people move efficiently with few delays on public transport. The rail networks of Japan's three largest metropolitan areas – Tokyo, Nagoya, and Osaka – are perhaps the most efficient in the world. The country's flagship high-speed line, the Tokaido Shinkansen, has operated for nearly 50 years without a single derailment or collision. Its average departure delay is less than a minute. Even more impressive than the few high-speed tracks is the complex web of metro and commuter lines, the result of a vibrant, free market in transportation. Singapore and Hong Kong also have private companies, but competition there is weak compared to Japan's array of independent firms, subject to restrictive price and other regulation.

After World War II, while nearly all railways and intra-city buses in Europe and North America were nationalized, Japan stayed its prewar course, with the railway industry retaining its few sizable private firms. Private railways proved to be more efficient than those run by the state, which were losing cash even in the dense Tokaido megalopolis. So, in 1987, the government privatized the Japanese National Railways, which operated every type of transit except trams and inner-city metros. JR East, JR Central, and JR West, the three spin-offs operating around Tokyo, Nagoya, and Osaka, respectively, emerged healthy and profitable. Privatization was later applied to Tokyo Metro, the largest subway network in the city.

Compare this to President Obama's high-speed rail project. Despite the administration spending nearly $11 billion since 2009 to develop faster passenger trains, the projects have gone mostly nowhere and the US still lags far behind Europe and China. Critics say that instead of putting the $11 billion directly into those projects, the administration made the mistake of parceling out the money to upgrade the existing Amtrak network, which will allow trains to go no faster than 110 mph. None of the money originally went to service in the northeast corridor, the most likely place for high-speed rail. On the crowded New York to Washington corridor, the Acela averages only 80 mph, and a plan to bring it up to the speed of Japanese bullet trains, which can top 220 mph, will take $150 billion and 26 years, if it ever happens.

In his 2011 State of the Union address, President Obama said: "Within 25 years, our goal is to give 80% of Americans access to high-speed rail." The Acela, introduced by Amtrak in 2000, was America's first successful high-speed train, and most days its cars are full. The train has reduced the time it takes to travel between Washington, New York, and Boston, but aging tracks and bridges – including Baltimore's 100-year-old tunnel where trains come to a crawl – have slowed it down. It takes 165 minutes to travel from New York to Washington on the Acela, instead of the 90 minutes it would take if it were a bullet train traveling on new tracks.

One problem is that Amtrak's funding is tied to annual appropriations from Congress, leaving it without a long-term source of money. After it was created in 1970, subsidies to Amtrak were supposed to be temporary, but this has not been the case, and Amtrak has provided a second-rate rail service for more than 30 years while consuming more than $30 billion in federal subsidies. It has a poor on-time record, and its infrastructure is in bad shape. Reforms elsewhere show that private passenger rail can work, but also that a public railway company can shape up considerably if it is professionally governed and exposed to competition. Such reforms have been implemented in Australia, Britain, Germany, Japan, New Zealand, and other countries.

This is not just a question of Amtrak's shortcomings and too little cash. Depressingly, much cash is poured into infrastructure projects that are poor investments. A good example of this is that many cities are building streetcar rails (also called trolleys or tramways), while rapid transit buses would be much cheaper and better. Washington DC spent at least $135 million to build streetcar rails that span 2.4 miles in the city's northeast.

At least 16 American cities have built similar systems, with dozens more in the works. Even bankrupt Detroit has begun work on a three-mile line of streetcar rails that is expected to cost $137 million. Most research finds that streetcars cost a multiple of what buses cost, without moving people more efficiently or more quickly. Their slow speeds and frequent stops mean they often cause more congestion. A bus route could move up to five times more people an hour.

An important reason why streetcar routes are being built is that federal subsidies have encouraged them. Under Barack Obama, the Department of Transportation has made grants of up to $75 million available to "small" projects that promise to revitalize urban areas and cut greenhouse gas emissions. They need not be cost-effective in the conventional sense if they make a place more livable or offer other vague benefits. This was not only wasteful, but tends to favor better-off riders, such as tourists and shoppers. Poorer residents would have been better served by buses. A positive example in this direction is Cleveland's rapid bus service that has attracted $5.8 billion in private investment along its 6.8-mile route. It was built in 2008 for around $50 million, a third of the cost of its streetcar.

In many cases, new infrastructure can be smartly financed by drawing on increasing land values. This only works for infrastructure investment that truly adds economic value to an area. A good example is the Crossrail project in the UK, an ambitious new railway line under central London connecting the southwest suburbs in Berkshire with Essex in the east. Due to be completed in 2018, it will increase the capacity of London's transport network by 10% and cut commuter traveling time significantly. Crossrail 1, estimated to cost £15 billion ($24 billion), is being financed by a combination of government grants, fares, and an enhancement of land values. Central government will supply around one-third and London businesses will contribute more than one-third, including from new development above the stations, and contributions from the key beneficiaries such as Heathrow Airport and the City of London. The remaining third (or less) will come from Transport for London, the local government body responsible for the transport system in Greater London, raised through borrowing and paid for through the Crossrail operating surplus. Network Rail will deliver works up to a value of £2.3 billion to enhance the existing rail network, paid back over 30 years through track access charges. The remainder primarily comes from the planned disposal of surplus land and property.[2, 3] Crossrail 2, the second phase of the project, is the proposed £20 billion rail line linking southwest and northeast London. More than half the cost could be met from sources other than the taxpayer.

Our examples have focused on railroads. But the story is similar in other infrastructure areas. Nearly all US seaports are owned by state and local governments. Many operate below world standards because of inflexible union work rules and administrative hang-ups. A Maritime Administration report noted that: "American ports lag well behind other international transportation gateways such as Singapore and Rotterdam." Inefficient ports are a definite hindrance to exports.

The privatization of ports has often been fairly successful. In Britain, 19 ports were privatized in 1983 to form Associated British Ports. Even in Greece, Pireaus is one of the few successful privatizations in Greece, where Cosco, albeit a Chinese SOE, bought half of the port and tripled turnover and efficiency in less than two years.[4] Hutchinson Whampoa, a private sector company based in Hong Kong, has been successful in taking over ports worldwide and now owns 30 ports in 15 countries.

Let NWFs shift state-owned assets toward infrastructure

A national wealth fund acting as a holding company for an SOE offers a politically easier way of shifting state assets toward infrastructure in a way that could achieve the aims of reducing governments' direct access to wealth, increasing funding of infrastructure, and putting infrastructure decisions on a sounder economic footing.

Some countries, like Canada, have a long history of pension funds investing in infrastructure. Since infrastructure investments are often large projects, these funds rarely invest more than 10% of their assets in infrastructure. Ironically, a number of SWFs are investing heavily in infrastructure – in countries other than their own. One famous example is Dubai Ports World, a company based in the United Arab Emirates, which in 2006 wanted to invest in six major ports in the US. This elicited concern that it could use its investments to influence shipping routes. In the end, Congress blocked Dubai Ports World's acquisition of the company that owned the ports, which had, to all intents and purposes, already taken place. Dubai Ports World eventually sold the American assets it had acquired to AIG.

Other examples include China Investment Corporation, the world's fourth largest SWF, which bought a 10% stake in Heathrow Airport Holdings, while the Qatar Investment Authority is reportedly considering using some of its $170 billion to build infrastructure in India. Meanwhile, Chinese companies are building roads and railways in Africa, power plants and bridges in Southeast Asia, and schools and bridges in America. In the most recent list of the world's biggest global contractors, compiled by an industry newsletter, *Engineering News-Record,* Chinese companies held four of the top twenty-five positions. China State Construction Engineering Corporation has undertaken more than 5,000 projects in about 100 different countries and earned $22.4 billion in revenues in 2009. China's Sinohydro controls more than half the world's market for building hydropower projects.

In fact, SWFs' and sometimes NWFs' investments in *other* countries' infrastructure have become so pervasive and apparently threatening that many countries have imposed discriminatory legal impediments against direct investments from these funds due to concerns about potential political motivations, so the regulatory hurdles they face are often much more onerous than for, say, pension funds. To address such concerns, SWFs have worked to improve their transparency by co-investing with pension funds and other funds with established international reputations.

Many of these countries have a great need for more domestic infrastructure investment. But there are limitations, not least governance issues that could result in the misuse of vast resources. However, many of these countries are still developing their intellectual and legal infrastructure, and this is where NWFs can help them do that by providing a window to international best practices and hands-on experience and management. SWFs are in a financial position to invest in large infrastructure projects, but an important issue is whether they have the competence that successful infrastructure investments require. Usually their expertise is financial, rather than structural.

In our view, national infrastructure investment can be boosted and managed better by letting an NWF shift or sell state assets in other commercial holdings and invest in infrastructure consortia in their own country. In doing so, three measures that reinforce each other are important.

First, an NWF that invests in infrastructure should have a focus on profitability and nothing else. Their job is to manage the value of operational assets, ensure economic soundness, and try to find structural deals that increase profitability. For example, many roads and railroad investments can become profitable if the increase in land value around these investments is internalized. An NWF is in a position to buy land surrounding such investments and thereby make projects profitable, or may indeed already be the owner through one of its holdings, such as the railways or the postal service.

Using an NWF to shift public assets toward infrastructure also helps politically. Governments often keep state enterprises merely because there is no strong political opinion for privatization. An NWF that, with some independence from the government, can, for example, sell a state-owned bank and invest in a profitable infrastructure project instead would not be seen as relinquishing net wealth to the private sector, but merely shifting wealth within its portfolio.

Second, infrastructure projects that are not commercially profitable, but have a positive net social value, should be paid for by state or local governments in the form of "payments for use." For example, a consortium owned by the NWF alone or together with private owners may make a contract with the state or a local government where the consortium builds a road, and the state commits to pay an annual usage fee that can vary depending on road accessibility and other quality parameters. This is already a common model in many public–private partnership (PPP) projects. For example, governments pay a PPP consortium annually for provision of a road or railroad often in relation to the quality the PPP achieves. That focuses governments on the value of a service to the consumer, rather than entangling them in difficult investment decisions that also offer temptations for corruption and clientelism. For example, the Lekki-Epe expressway close to Lagos in Nigeria is being built as a PPP project, avoiding much of the corruption common in the country's other infrastructure projects.

Third, an independent institute should continually evaluate the social profitability of infrastructure services that governments purchase. For this they should use internationally accepted tools to determine how to factor in environmental and social values. While the recommendations of such an independent institute can probably not be made binding, it would make the economic rationale for various projects more transparent, and impose a political cost on governments that invest in bridges to nowhere.

Smarter infrastructure

An NWF is also well placed to innovate financing of infrastructure through value generation. For example, highways are often flagrant examples of missed opportunities. A number of US states have built, or are building, privately financed and operated highways. The Dulles Greenway in Northern Virginia is a 14-mile private highway opened in 1995 that was financed by private bond and equity issues. In the same region, Fluor-Transurban is building and mainly funding toll lanes on a 14-mile stretch of the Capital Beltway. Drivers will pay to use the lanes with electronic tolling, which will recoup the $1 billion investment. Fluor-Transurban is also financing and building toll lanes running south from Washington along Interstate 95. Similar private highway projects have been completed, or are being pursued, in California, Maryland, Minnesota, North Carolina, South Carolina, and Texas.

Yet, the main opportunity does not lie in charging tolls for individual roads. Rather, it lies in overall value creation in connection with highways. Unlike most other physical assets, land can be a vehicle for managed capital appreciation, particularly when governments themselves are the primary source of allocating development rights and constructing the public infrastructure required to add value. When public authorities open up new land by building roads, providing infrastructure services, or relocating public offices, they create incremental land values, sometimes of great magnitude. When public authorities own the land in question, a shrewd infrastructure investment strategy, coupled with changes in the land use designation, can recapture large portions of the costs of capital investment, and in some cases the entirety of costs, from land value appreciation and subsequent land sales. For example, in Changsha,

add benefits

the capital of Hunan Province in China, more than half the finance for an eight-lane ring road came from the sale of publicly owned adjacent land (and interim borrowing against the value of the land parcels).

Another type of value creation lies in creating a toll system to relieve congestion. Instead of charging for access to individual highways or bridges, a well-managed transport system would introduce higher tolls during rush hour in order to reduce congestion. This has proved unexpectedly successful in Stockholm, for example. The city government introduced a charge for cars driving during peak traffic hours that led to a 20% reduction in rush-hour traffic. Most of the city's residents were initially opposed to the fee, but now 70% of the population support the congestion charge.

In Germany, which has crowded highways and restrictions on public financing, Finance Minister Wolfgang Schäuble recently suggested a general highway toll, which would be collected with electronic devices, without the need for expensive tolling stations, which would reduce queues by evening out traffic flows between peak and nonpeak hours, while raising finance from users.

Even for local transport, congestion charges appear to work. London, for example, introduced the congestion charge in 2003, which operates in central London from 7 am to 6 pm, Monday to Friday. Several studies show that these charges help to reduce congestion, mainly by inducing some travelers to avoid rush hour. In the first ten years of the scheme in London, gross revenue was £2.6 billion, while around £1.2 billion of net revenue (46%) was invested in public transport and walking and cycling schemes.

In many countries, such changes to fee structures for consumers, or fees that transport operators pay for the use of rails and other infrastructure, are subject to intense political haggling. In many cases, these kinds of decisions could probably be made more rationally if they were spearheaded by public infrastructure consortia under the auspices of an NWF.

An interesting development, possibly in that direction, is taking place for Network Rail, the state-backed organization that owns and operates Britain's railway infrastructure. The EU is demanding that Britain either reclassify Network Rail's £34 billion of gross debts as public debt, or turn

Network Rail into an independent body. Network Rail, which controls 2,500 stations, railway tracks, tunnels, bridges and level crossings, was set up in 2002 as a private company with no shareholders, but with its finances guaranteed by the government. It has occasionally been fined by the Office of Rail Regulation for failing to meet train punctuality targets. The logical step, in line with our argument, would be to convert Network Rail into an independent entity owned by an NWF.

In sum, there is great scope for more efficient provision of public infrastructure, and many countries have good reason to shift public assets from the SOEs that lack good reasons for state ownership toward infrastructure. An NWF provides a politically feasible vehicle for such a shift. In addition, such a politically independent fund can introduce an element of economic rationality in infrastructure investments.

14

From decay to governance in the public interest

Francis Fukuyama (2014a) provides a lucid account of the failings of state governance in his essay "America in decay." Many of his observations corroborate our description of how state-owned wealth is mismanaged in many countries. Fukuyama writes:

> Distrust of government then perpetuates and feeds on itself. Distrust of executive agencies leads to demands for more legal checks on administration, which reduces the quality and effectiveness of government. At the same time demand for government services induces Congress to impose new mandates on the executive, which often prove difficult, if not impossible, to fulfill. Both processes lead to a reduction of bureaucratic autonomy, which in turn leads to rigid, rule-bound, uncreative and incoherent government.

> The result is a crisis of representation, in which ordinary citizens feel that their supposedly democratic government no longer truly reflects their interests and is under the control of shadowy elites. What is ironic and peculiar about this phenomenon is that this crisis of representation has occurred in large part because of reforms designed to make the system more democratic. In fact, these days there is too much law and too much democracy relative to American state capacity.

This analysis mirrors our argument on governance of public wealth. Sadly, Fukuyama offers little hope other than that the prospect of a coming crisis may spur reforms. Our view is slightly more sanguine. A reform process of small steps is possible and some countries are actually beating the path. Through these steps, politicians can relinquish direct access to public wealth, and thus help to focus their minds on the lot of the people. The parallel history of central banks and public pension funds shows that enlightened politicians may come to choose this reform path of their own accord and even in the absence of a crisis.

The gist of our argument also cuts through the phony war that has long raged between those in favor of the public ownership of commercial assets and those against – privatization versus nationalization. What matters most is the quality of asset governance.

The fact that the value of most countries' public assets exceeds their public debt has been overlooked because governments seldom have a complete understanding of their portfolio. If anything, our method tends to underestimate asset value since governments lack a central registry and the proper accounting to assess the market value of these assets.

Transparency is a key to better management. With a consolidated understanding of the value and breakdown of the portfolio of public commercial assets, it is not difficult to improve the yield, be it of state-owned firms, real estate, productive forests, or other public assets that provide some kind of income stream.

The lack of efficiency and financial return among public commercial assets is confirmed in a wide variety of case studies, ranging from Fukuyama's penetrating exposé of the management of state-owned forests in the US to the Lithuanian government's discovery of its own inefficient forests. In this book, we have given many examples from banking, energy firms, airlines, and many other sectors in rich and poor countries.

The most challenging feat required of state ownership is that government must ultimately be both player and referee, both market participant and regulator. This duality needs to be addressed head on through a legally clear separation between ownership and governance. Ministers should only be able to influence a sector and its participants through transparent and fair regulation.

Our common resources are limited. It is therefore imperative that they are managed responsibly. Public commercial assets that remain hidden, without a transparent economic value, risk being misused without anyone paying much attention. An understanding of value, both current and potential, is fundamental to the development of any commercial asset. Transparency is also crucial to prevent waste, misuse, and corruption of public assets.

Some countries have taken steps to increase transparency by monetizing their assets, or are planning to do so. Even a socialist country like Vietnam is trying to clean up its SOEs by selling off noncore assets, and plans to cut their total number by 75% by 2020. In India, most policy makers say they want to break up Coal India to boost competition. Yet this is only the beginning. Even after such changes, most governments will still have vast assets on their hands.

Instead, if public commercial assets were vested in a national wealth fund, the time-proven tools and frameworks of the private sector and professional governance can boost public wealth. An NWF would require a ring-fenced corporate vehicle owning all commercial assets at arm's length from short-term political influence.

Politicians would be more successful if they focused solely on issues concerning individual citizens and the economy as a whole. Most governments have already outsourced the management of monetary and financial stability to independent central banks, and passed control of pension funds to professional fund managers. Following this lead, establishing a more professional solution for our public commercial assets including public real estate through an NWF is the logical next step. Many countries, especially those with highly devolved federal systems of government, will probably need NWFs at the regional and local level as well.

The current economic situation in Europe and the US as well as many other developed economies of the OECD requires extraordinary measures. Governments responsible for the ownership of commercial assets share the same challenges. None can ever be an ideal owner due to the inherent conflict of interest. Yet, it should be incumbent on all decision makers to allow for such assets to be managed professionally and to do so in the interests of all citizens, however unpopular that may be with some vested interests. A public reform program for the governance of public wealth is a financial and social enterprise with a huge upside for public finances, democracy, and the ongoing battle against corruption.

Notes

Chapter 1

1   According to Kowalski et al. (2013). Based on firm-level ownership data and considering direct and indirect ownership.

2   IMF (2013).

3   GAO (2005); see Managing Federal Real Property.

4   Based on our estimate of global public commercial assets totaling US$75 trillion.

5   Spending on global basic infrastructure according to the World Economic Forum.

6   Peterson (1985).

7   Tanzi and Prakash (2000).

8   As proposed by Buiter (1983).

9   Nicholas Lardy (2014) of the Peterson Institute for International Economics argues convincingly that it is the private sector, not SOEs, that have powered the country's growth since the country's reform era began in 1978.

10   Murray et al. (2013).

11   Myrdal (1968).

12   Fölster and Sanandaji (2014).

13   For example, Herle and Springford (2010).

Chapter 2

1   Several European countries had authoritarian regimes until the mid-1970s, including Greece (1974), Spain (1975), and Portugal (1974). All Eastern Europe was effectively under Soviet communist control until 1991, including Romania (1989) and Eastern Germany until 1990. The break-up of Yugoslavia from the former communist regime and the ensuing ethnic war lasted most of the 1990s, with several states reaching official independence only in the 2000s, such as Serbia, Montenegro (2006), and Kosovo (2008).

2   See Lardy (2014).

3   In dollars since 2007, depending on how one treats firms that were unlisted at the start of the period. According to *The Economist* (2014a).

4   *Financial Times* (2014) "Lenovo to buy IBM server unit for US$2.3 billion", January 23.

5   *Wall Street Journal* (2014) "Lenovo completes Motorola acquisition", October 30.
6   McGregor (2012).
7   Lardy (2014).
8   Netter and Megginson (2001) provide a good review of this literature.
9   Kim and Chung (2008).
10   Bartel and Harrison (1999).
11   Bloom and van Reenen (2010) and Bloom et al. (2012) describe the double-blind survey techniques and randomized sampling used to construct management data over many types of organization and countries.
12   Kapopoulos and Lazaretou (2005).
13   These were listed and nonlisted firms and statutory corporations.
14   Persons per 100,000 inhabitants who start college education.

Chapter 3

1   Liu and Mikesell (2014). The question of causation is not fully explored in these studies, and is also conceptually complicated. For example, it could be that industry structure or cultural norms or institutions are more basic drivers of both corruption and state intervention.
2   According to *The Economist*, "Politics and the purse", September 19, 2013, www.economist.com/blogs/graphicdetail/2013/09/daily-chart-14.
3   Edwards (2004).
4   Lardy (2014).
5   Common Cause (2008).
6   *Süddeutsche Zeitung* in a series of articles during 2010.
7   Fukuyama (2014a).

Chapter 4

1   *The Economist* (2014) "The $9 Trillion Sale", January 11.
2   Grubišic et al. (2009).
3   *The New York Times* (2013) "Who owns this land? In Greece, who knows?", May 26.
4   Grubišic et al. (2009).
5   Accounts for 2013.
6   Office for National Statistics (2012) *The National Balance Sheet.*
7   HM Treasury (2014) *Whole of Government Accounts, 2012 to 2014.*
8   HM Treasury (2007) *National Asset Register.*
9   Audit Commission (2014) *Managing Council Property Assets.* The reason the numbers are different from those of public sector net debt (PSND) is because WGA is using IFRS and has a wider scope than PSND, most notably because of the inclusion of fixed assets such as property, plant and equipment, and public service pension liabilities.
10   Manning (2012).
11   Baber (2011).
12   Buiter (1983).

13 See, for example, IMF (2013).

14 Nonproduced assets are included for only 16 of the 27 countries in the IMF data.

15 One of these countries is Ukraine, which is described further in the next section. Another country is Sweden. Our estimate for Sweden follows a calculation done by PwC of real estate value based on taxation values. The value of SOEs owned by the central government is taken from the Swedish government's annual report for 2013, valued at SEK 500 billion. In addition, PwC arrived at real estate and utilities' net value of US$20 billion. All in all, nonfinancial assets for Sweden are valued at US$230 billion.

16 We estimated regressions that explain the size of financial and nonfinancial public assets as a function of GDP, the population size, a measure of democracy, a measure of natural resource endowments, and gross debt. The coefficient estimates of these regressions are then used to calculate a predicted value of public assets for each country. This way of extrapolating to world public assets takes better account of structural differences between the countries for which we have public asset figures and those for which we do not.

17 PwC (2013).

18 According to the World Bank, total reserves in 2013 (includes gold, current US$).

19 Worldwide national wealth funds and their assets are listed in Table 10.1.

20 According to Credit Suisse (2014), world household wealth amounts to US$263 trillion, of which about half is financial and most of the rest is real estate.

21 For example, Bom and Ligthart (2010).

22 According to estimates by GaveKal Dragonomics, a Beijing-based economic research house. These numbers may not be strictly comparable. It is possible that private returns include the benefit of public services not being priced. Once these are properly priced, the returns on public assets would increase, but those on private assets may decrease. Rent seeking is a clear example of this: the private sector gets a return that actually belongs to taxpayers.

23 Statoil is valued much higher in spite of the fact that its deep sea oil and gas fields involve high extraction costs.

24 *The Economist* (2014b).

25 World Bank (2011).

26 Including budget contribution from state asset dividends of approximately 0.2% of GDP, fiscal support through budget transfers of resources totaled 2% of GDP, energy subsidies both on and off budget, exceeding 7.5% of GDP in 2012. Built-up arrears by Naftogaz of some $2.2 billion, or 1.5% of GDP to Gazprom (Ukraine Ministry of Finance, 2013). An additional 1% of GDP in added costs in a supplementary budget for additional capital that might be needed to prop up the banking sector (IMF, 2014).

27 Ukrainian Ministry of Finance.

28 IMF (2012).

29 Accounting Chamber of Ukraine (2009).

30 For example, Robinson et al. (2005), Tanzi and Davoodi (2000), or Sawyer (2010).

31 Gupta et al. (2011).

32 *The New York Times* (2011) "Time Warner trims its excesses", October 31.

33 Swedish Government (2011) and company annual reports.

34 Senate Properties, www.senaatti.fi/en.

35   ETAD was created in late 2011 from the merger of two pre-existing state entities – the Hellenic Public Real Estate Corporation (KED) and the Hellenic Tourist Properties (ETA). KED was established in 1979 as the maintenance arm of the Ministry of Finance and has been used as the management company for real estate assets, involving the registration of property and the development of the land registry and the assets. ETA was the equivalent maintenance arm, which managed the real estate assets of the Ministry of Tourism.

36   The US Civilian Property Alignment Act 2012 (H.R. 1734).

37   Ibid.

Chapter 5

1   See Walker (2003).

2   Lithuanian Government (2009); Latvian Government (2009).

3   Lithuanian Government (2009).

4   Haldane and Madouros (2012).

Chapter 6

1   See, for example, Megginson et al. (2004).

2   See OECD (1998). More recent changes in state control appear to be focused on lifting price controls rather than privatization.

3   Bloomberg (2010) "Petrobras raises $70 billion in world's largest share sale", September 24.

4   Reuters (2014) "Brazil's Petrobras faces another lawsuit over corruption scandal", December 15.

Chapter 7

1   *Financial Times* (1999) "Sweden lets its champions go", January 29.

2   UBS Warburg (2000) "Privatisation international, Sweden: bold, novel approach", December.

3   Carnegie (2002a).

4   Merrill Lynch (2000).

5   *Financial Times* (1999) "Swedish government hires financiers", June 1.

6   At such a point in time, prior to the actual appointment, a minister-to-be appointed is likely to submit to such a concession.

7   Swedish Government (2005).

8   Ibid.

9   Carnegie (2002b).

10   BNP Paribas (2001).

11   SEKO (2000).

12   Swedish Government (2000).

13   *Financial Times* (1999) "Welcome to the ways of the market", November 12.

14   Ibid.

15   Swedish Government (2004).

16   Merrill Lynch (2000).

17   JP Morgan (2000).

18   UBS Warburg (2000).

19   Swedish Government (2005).

20   Swedish Government (2012).

21   *Financial Times* (2013) "Writedown moves Vattenfall to restructure", July 23.

22   *Financial Times* (2014) "Utilities companies search for new business models as losses mount", October 22.

23   *Financial Times* (2013), op. cit.

24   *Financial Times* (2009) "Vattenfall lands Nuon in €8.5 billion deal", February 24.

Chapter 8

1   Finnish Government (2004).

2   Norwegian Government (2002).

3   OECD (2005a).

4   Useem (1993) gives a telling account of this change.

5   For example, Alesina and Summers (1993).

6   See, for example, Iglesias and Palacios (2000).

7   Goh (1972).

8   Ng (2009).

9   House Financial Services Committee (2008).

10   Low (2004).

11   Under the Willow Tree (2011).

12   IMF (2003).

13   Shome (2006).

14   Ng (2009).

15   House Financial Services Committee (2008).

16   *Wall Street Journal* (2009) "At Temasek, a foreign CEO-to-be won't", July 22.

17   *The Guardian* (2009) "Temasek abandons plan to install Chip Goodyear as chief executive", July 21.

18   Ibid.

19   *Financial Times* (2014) "Temasek's dealmaking reflects big bets on the rise of the consumer", April 14.

20   *Financial Times* (2014) "Temasek widens its Africa footprint", April 15.

21   Temasek (2014) *Annual Review*.

22   Balding (2011).

23   Shome (2006).

24   Temasek (2014), op. cit.

25   Ibid.

26 Temasek (2010) $10m MTN Program, February 3.

27 Lardy (2014).

Chapter 9

1 *Financial Times* (2014) "Corruption with Chinese characteristics", August 12.

2 Fukuyama (2014b).

3 Buiter (1983).

4 Tanzi et al. (2000).

5 Swedish Government (2007).

6 Solidium (2013).

7 *Financial Times* (1999) "Welcome to the ways of the market", November 12.

8 OECD (2005a).

9 Micklethwait and Wooldridge (2014).

10 Olson (1982).

11 *The Economist* (2011) "The East India Company: the Company that ruled the waves", December 17.

Chapter 10

1 Shleifer and Vishny (1997).

2 Cadbury Report (1992).

3 Verhoeven et al. (2008).

4 *Financial Times* (2014) "China slowdown threatens timetable for financial reform", September 28.

5 OECD (2005a).

6 Assemblée Nationale (2003).

7 Rozanov (2005).

8 Nicolas et al. (2014).

9 SWF Institute website: www.swfinstitute.org.

10 Wicaksono (2009).

11 "Stubb: Hands off Solidium", January 25, 2014, http://yle.fi/uutiset/stubb_hands_off_solidium/7052254.

12 McKinsey & Co (2006).

13 *The Economist* (2013) "The world's biggest banks", July 13.

14 Forbes (2013) "World's largest corporations in 2013", July 7.

Chapter 11

1 Institute for Government (2012).

2 Eleftheriadis (2014).

3 Annington and Terra Firma websites.

4   Choosing debt or equity does not matter in a world without distortions and liquidity constraints, but the government itself has introduced a distortion by making debt interest deductable and equity dividends not. This notion is slowly being reconsidered in modern tax policy analysis.

5   HM Treasury (2010).

6   Parker (2012).

7   *Financial Times* (2013) "Rail to Royal Mail: the dangers of flawed privatisations", October 10.

8   Naughton (2007).

9   Ibid.

10 Ibid.

Chapter 12

1   Bagehot (1873).

2   OECD (2005b).

3   Unger (2006).

4   In practice, the Organization Department appoints the party committee within each state-owned asset/bank. Because the chairmen of the party committee must be given a senior role, they tend to be appointed as the executive chairmen. The faren, being the legally responsible person, is typically much less significant.

5   Swedish Government (2004). Contains the complete guidelines for external financial reporting adopted by the government on March 21, 2002 and the guidelines for terms of employment and incentive schemes adopted by the government on October 9, 2003.

6   Crowe and Meade (2007).

7   The Sveriges Riksbank Act (1988:1385), available at www.riksbank.se/en/The-Riksbank/Legislation/The-Sveriges-Riksbank-Act/.

8   Bachmann (2001).

9   DeConick (2010).

10 Goddard (2003).

Chapter 13

1   Unless they render a revenue stream, such as toll roads.

2   London First (2014).

3   *The Economist* (2013) "How other infrastructure projects can learn from London's new railway", November 23.

4   *The New York Times* (2012) "Chinese company sets new rhythm in port of Piraeus", October 10.

References

Accounting Chamber of Ukraine (2009) Audit of "Naftogaz Ukrainy". Kiev.

Alesina, A. and Summers, L.H. (1993) "Central bank independence and macroeconomic performance: some comparative evidence", *Journal of Money, Credit and Banking*, 25(2): 151–62.

Assemblée Nationale (2003) "Rapport fait au nom de la commission d'enquête sur la gestion des entreprises publiques afin d'améliorer le système de prise de décision", Rapport Douste-Blazy, N° 1004. (Paris).

Baber, B. (2011) "Squeezing the assets", May 1, available at www.publicfinance.co.uk/features/2011/05/squeezing-the-assets.

Bachmann, R. (2001) "Trust, power and control in transorganizational relations", *Organization Studies*, 22(2): 337–65.

Bagehot, W. (1873) *Lombard Street: A Description of the Money Market.* (New York: Scribner, Armstong & Co.).

Balding, C. (2011) *A Brief Research Note on Temasek Holdings and Singapore: Mr. Madoff Goes to Singapore*, available at piketty.pse.ens.fr/files/Balding13.pdf.

Bartel, A. and Harrison, A. (1999) *Ownership versus Environment: Why are Public Sector Firms Inefficient?*, NBER Working Paper No. 7043.

Bloom, N. and van Reenen, J. (2010) "Why do management practices differ across firms and countries?", *Journal of Economic Perspectives*, 24(1): 203–24.

Bloom, N., Genakos, C., Sadun, R. and van Reenen, J. (2012) *Management Practices across Firms and Countries*, NBER Working Paper No. 17850.

BNP Paribas (2001) *Sweden: Blazing the Reform Trail*, June 21. (London: BNP Paribas).

Bom, P. and Ligthart, J.E. (2010) "What have we learned from three decades of research on the productivity of public capital?", CESifo Working Paper Series No. 2206, Center Discussion Paper No. 2008–10.

Buiter, W.H. (1983) "Measurement of the public sector deficit and its implications for policy evaluation and design", *Staff Papers*, IMF, 30: 306–49.

Cadbury Report (1992) *Report of the the Committee on the Financial Aspects of Corporate Governance.* (London: Gee Publishing).

Carnegie (2002a) *Case Study: AssiDomän*, March 1.

Carnegie (2002b) *From an Integrated State Railroad Authority to a Structure with Specialised Corporate Entities,* June 1.

Christiansen, H. (2011) *The Size and Composition of the SOE Sector in OECD Countries,* OECD Corporate Governance Working Papers, No. 5. (OECD Publishing).

Common Cause (2008) "Ask Yourself Why ... They Didn't See This Coming", available at www.commoncause.org/.../National_092408_Education_Fund_ Report (accessed September 29, 2008).

Credit Suisse (2014) *Global Wealth Report 2014.*

Crowe, C. and Meade, E.E. (2007) "The evolution of central bank governance around the world", *Journal of Economic Perspectives,* 21(4): 69–90.

DeConick, J.B. (2010) "The effect of organizational justice, perceived organizational support, and perceived supervisor support on marketing employees' level of trust", *Journal of Business Research,* 63(12): 1349–55.

Economist, The (2014a) "State capitalism in the dock", November 22.

Economist, The (2014b) "Our crony-capitalism index", March 15.

Edwards, J.R. (2004) "How nineteenth-century Americans responded to government corruption", *The Freeman: Ideas on Liberty,* April, p. 24.

Eleftheriadis, P. (2014) "Misrule of the few: how the oligarchs ruined Greece", *Foreign Affairs,* 93(6): 139–46.

Finnish Government (2004) *Matti Vuoria: Evaluator Report of the State's Ownership Policy.* (Helsinki, Prime Minister's Office).

Fölster, O. and Sanandaji, N. (2014) *Renaissance for Reforms.* (London: IEA/ Timbro).

Fukuyama, F. (2014a) "America in decay: the sources of political dysfunction", *Foreign Affairs,* 93(5): 763–75.

Fukuyama, F. (2014b) *Political Order and Political Decay: From the Industrial Revolution to the Globalization of Democracy.* (New York: Farrar, Strauss and Giroux).

GAO (General Accounting Office) (2005) *High-Risk Series: An Update,* GAO-05-207.

Goddard, R. (2003) "Relation network, social trust, and norms: a social capitol perspective on students' chances of academic success", *Educational Evaluation and Policy Analysis,* 25(1): 59–74.

Goel, R. and Nelson, M.A. (1998) "Corruption and government size: a disaggregated analysis", *Public Choice,* 97(1/2): 107–20.

Goh, K.S. (1972) *The Economics of Modernisation and Other Essays.* (Singapore: Asia Pacific Press).

Grubišić, M., Nušinović, M. and Roje, G. (2009) "Towards efficient public sector asset management", *Financial Theory and Practice*, 33(3): 329–62.

Gupta, S., Kangur, A., Papageorgiou, C. and Wane, A. (2011) *Efficiency-adjusted Public Capital and Growth*, IMF Working Paper WP/11/217.

Haldane, A. and Madouros, V. (2012) "The Dog and the Frisbee", paper presented at the Federal Reserve Bank of Kansas City's 36th economic policy symposium.

Haley, U. and Haley, G. (2013) *Subsidies to Chinese Industry: State Capitalism, Business Strategy, and Trade Policy*. (Oxford: Oxford University Press).

Herle, D. and Springford, J. (2010) "Prairie wisdom for Britain's age of austerity", *Financial Times*, June 9.

HM Treasury (2010) *Joint Venture Guidance*, available at www.hm-treasury.gov.uk/d/joint_venture_guidance.pdf.

House Financial Services Committee (2008) *Temasek Holdings: A Dependable Investor in the United States*, testimony of Simon Israel, March 5, available at www.temasek.com.sg/mediacentre/speeches?detailid=8609.

Iglesias, A. and Palacios, R.J. (2000) *Managing Public Pension Reserves. Part I: Evidence from the International Experience.* (Washington: Social Protection Unit, World Bank).

IMF (International Monetary Fund) (2003) *Singapore Inc. vs the Private Sector: Are GLCs Different?* (Washington DC: IMF).

IMF (2004) *World Economic Outlook.* (Washington DC: IMF).

IMF (2012) *Ukraine Gas Pricing Policy: Distributional Consequences of Tariff Increases*, Working Paper 12/247. (Washington DC: IMF).

IMF (2013) *Another Look at Governments' Balance Sheets: The Role of Nonfinancial Assets.* IMF Working Paper 13/95. (Washington DC: IMF).

IMF (2014) *World Economic Outlook: Legacies, Clouds, Uncertainties.* (Washington DC: IMF).

Institute for Government (2012) *The "S" Factors: Lessons from IFG's Policy Success Reunions.* (London: Institute for Government).

JP Morgan (2000) Posten AB, Productivity has been delivered, but the check is still in the mail, January.

Kim, J. and Chung, H. (2008) *Empirical Study on the Performance of State-owned-enterprises and the Privatizing Pressure: The Case of Korea.* (Graduate School of Public Administration, Seoul National University, Korea).

Kowalski, P., Büge, M., Sztajerowska, M. and Egeland, M. (2013) *State-owned Enterprises: Trade Effects and Policy Implications*, OECD Trade Policy Paper, No. 147. (OECD Publishing).

Kapopoulos, P. and Lazaretou, S. (2005) *Does Corporate Ownership Structure Matter for Economic Growth? A Cross-country Analysis*, Working Paper 21. (Bank of Greece, Economic Research Department).

Lardy, N. (2014) *Markets over Mao: The Rise of Private Business in China.* (Washington DC: Peterson Institute for International Economics).

Latvian Government (2009) *Annual Review Latvian State-owned Assets 2009.* (Riga, Nasdaq OMX).

Lithuanian Government (2009) *Annual Review State-Owned Commercial Assets 2009.* (Ministry of Economics, Vilnius).

Liu, C. and Mikesell, J.L. (2014) "The impact of public officials' corruption on the size and allocation of U.S. state spending", *Public Administration Review*, 74(3): 346–59.

London First (2014) *Funding Crossrail 2: A Report from London First's Task Force on Funding Crossrail 2.* (London: London First).

Low, L. (2004) "Singapore's developmental state between a rock and a hard place", in Low, L. (ed.) *Developmental States: Relevancy, Redundancy or Reconfiguration.* (Hauppauge, NY: Nova Science).

McGregor, R. (2012) *The Party: The Secret World of China's Communist Rulers* (2nd edn). (New York: Harper Perennial).

McKinsey & Co (2006) "The promise and perils of the Chinese banking system". Available at www.mckinsey.com/insights/financial_services/the_promise_and_perils_of_chinas_banking_system.

Manning, J. (2012) *More Light More Power: Reimagining Public Asset Management.* (London: New Local Government Network).

Megginson, W.L., Nash, R.C., Netter, J.M. and Poulson, A.B. (2004) "The choice of private versus public capital markets: evidence from privatizations", *The Journal of Finance*, 59(6): 2835–70.

Merrill Lynch (2000) *Sweden: Ripe for "New Economy" Gains*, September 4.

Micklethwait, J. and Wooldridge, A. (2014) *The Fourth Revolution: The Global Race to Reinvent the State.* (New York: Penguin Press).

Murray, C.J., Vos, T., Lozano, R. et al. (2013) "Disability-adjusted life years (DALYs) for 291 diseases and injuries in 21 regions, 1990–2010: a systematic analysis for the Global Burden of Disease Study 2010", *Lancet*, 380(9859): 2197–223.

Musacchio, A. and Lazzarini, S.G. (2014) *Reinventing State Capitalism: Leviathan in Business: Brazil and Beyond.* (Boston: Harvard University Press).

Musacchio, A., Pineda-Ayerbe, E. and García, G. (2015) "State-owned enterprise reform in Latin America: issues and solutions", mimeo, Inter-American Development Bank, February.

Myrdal, G. (1968) *Asian Drama: An Inquiry into the Poverty of Nations.* (New York: Pantheon).

Naughton, B.J. (2007) *The Chinese Economy: Transitions and Growth.* (Cambridge, MA: MIT Press).

Netter, J.M. and Megginson, W.L. (2001) "From state to market: a survey of empirical studies on privatization", *Journal of Economic Literature*, 39(2): 321–89.

Ng, W. (2009) "The evolution of sovereign wealth funds: Singapore's Temasek", *Journal of Financial Regulation and Compliance*, 18(1): 6–14.

Nicolas, M., Firzli, J. and Franzel, J. (2014) "Non-federal sovereign wealth funds in the United States and Canada", *Revue Analyse Financière*, Q3.

Norwegian Government (2002) *Reduced and Improved State Ownership*, White Paper. (Oslo, Stortinget).

OECD (Organisation for Economic Co-operation and Development) (1998) *Performance and Regulatory Patterns in OECD Countries*, ECO/CPE/WP1 (98)15.

OECD (2005a) *Guidelines on Corporate Governance of State-owned Enterprises.* (OECD Publishing).

OECD (2005b) *Corporate Governance of State-owned Enterprises: A Survey of OECD Countries.* (OECD Publishing).

OECD (2014) *Foreign Bribery Report: An Analysis of the Crime of Bribery of Foreign Public Officials.* (OECD Publishing).

Olson, M. (1982) *The Rise and Decline of Nations: Economic Growth, Stagflation and Social Rigidities.* (New Haven: Yale University Press).

Parker, D. (2012) *The Official History of Privatisation,* vol. 2. (London: Routledge).

Peterson, E. (1985) *Panama: Urban Development Assessment.* (Washington DC: The Urban Institute).

PwC (2013) *Asset Management 2020: A Brave New World.*

Robinson, J.A., Acemoglu, D. and Johnson, S. (2005) "Institutions as a fundamental cause of long-run growth", *Handbook of Economic Growth*, 1A, 386–472.

Rozanov, A. (2005) "Who holds the wealth of nations?", *Central Banking Journal*, 15(4): 52–7.

Sassoon, J. and Pellbäck, M. (2000) "Sweden: bold novel approach", *Privatisation International*, December 1, 8–10.

Sawyer, C.W. (2010) "Institutional quality and economic growth in Latin America", *Global Economy Journal*, 10(4): 1–13.

Shleifer, A. and Vishny, R.W. (1997) "A survey of corporate governance", *The Journal of Finance*, 52(20): 737–8.

Shome, A. (2006) *A Case Study of Positive Interventionism*, Working Paper. (Massey University, New Zealand).

SEKO (2000) *SEKO and Ownership: Casting off the Yoke of Monopoly and Entering a New Era.* (Stockholm).

Solidium (2013) *Annual Report*, available at www.e-julkaisu.fi/solidium/annualreport-2013/.

Swedish Government (2000) *Ownership Policy: Government-owned Companies* (Ministry of Industry, Employment and Communications).

Swedish Government (2004) *State Ownership Policy.*

Swedish Government (2005) *Liberalisering, regler och marknade (Liberalization, Regulation and Markets).* (Stockholm, SOU 2005, 4).

Swedish Government (2007) *Guidelines for External Reporting by State-owned Companies.* (Stockholm).

Swedish Government (2011) *Statens som fastighetsägare och hyresgäst (State as Landlords and Tenants).* (Stockholm, SOU 2011, 31).

Swedish Government (2012) *Ekonomiskt värde och samhällsnytta:* förslag till en ny statlig ägarförvaltning (*Economic Value and Social Benefit: Proposal for a New Governmental Ownership and Administration*). (Stockholm, SOU 2012, 14).

Tanzi, V. and Davoodi, H.R. (2000) *Corruption, Growth, and Public Finances*, IMF Working Paper 00/182.

Tanzi, V. and Prakash, T. (2000) *The Cost of Government and the Misuse of Public Funds*, IMF Working Paper 00/180.

UBS Warburg (2000) *Global Equity Research: Telia: Ready for Lift-Off*, July 18.

Under the Willow Tree (2011) "Wikileaks' stunning revelations about Singapore's corporate elite", September 4. Available at http://utwt.blogspot.co.uk/2011/09/wikileaks-stunning-revelations-about.html.

Unger, S. (2006) *Special Features of Swedish Corporate Governance.* (Stockholm: Swedish Corporate Governance Board).

Verhoeven, M., le Borgne, E., Medas, P. and Jones, L. (2008) *Assessing Fiscal Risk from State-Owned Enterprises.* (Washington DC: IMF).

Walker, D.M. (2003) "Federal Real Property: Actions Needed to Address Long-standing and Complex Problems", GAO report no. 04-119T. Testimony before the Committee on Governmental Affairs, United States Senate, October 1.

Wicaksono, A. (2009) Corporate governance of state-owned enterprises: investment holding structure of government-linked companies in Singapore and Malaysia and applicability for Indonesian state-owned enterprises, dissertation. (University of St. Gallen, Switzerland).

World Bank (2011) *Ukraine: System of Financial Oversight and Governance of State-Owned Enterprises*, Report No.: 59950, February 22.

Index

Printed and bound by CPI Group (UK) Ltd, Croydon, CR0 4YY